PENGUIN PASSNOTES

Henry IV, Part I

Peter J. Connor was educated at Leeds University where
he read English and Philosophy. After working
abroad for a year he took his postgraduate Certificate
of Education at Manchester. He now teaches at a tutorial
college in London.

PENGUIN PASSNOTES

WILLIAM SHAKESPEARE
Henry IV, Part I

PETER J. CONNOR
ADVISORY EDITOR: S. H. COOTE, M.A., PH.D.

PENGUIN BOOKS

Penguin Books Ltd, Harmondsworth, Middlesex, England
Penguin Books, 40 West 23rd Street, New York, New York 10010, U.S.A.
Penguin Books Australia Ltd, Ringwood, Victoria, Australia
Penguin Books Canada Ltd, 2801 John Street, Markham, Ontario, Canada L3R 1B4
Penguin Books (N.Z.) Ltd, 182–190 Wairau Road, Auckland 10, New Zealand

First published 1984

Made and printed in Great Britain by
Richard Clay (The Chaucer Press) Ltd, Bungay, Suffolk
Filmset in Monophoto Ehrhardt by Northumberland Press Ltd, Gateshead

*The publishers are grateful to the following Examination Boards for
permission to reproduce questions from examination papers used in
individual titles in the Passnotes series:*

*Associated Examining Board, University of Cambridge Local Examinations
Syndicate, Joint Matriculation Board, University of London School
Examinations Department, Oxford and Cambridge Schools Examination
Board, University of Oxford Delegacy of Local Examinations.*

*The Examination Boards accept no responsibility whatsoever for the
accuracy or method of working in any suggested answers given as models.*

Contents

To the Student

This book is designed to help you with your O-level or C.S.E. English Literature examinations. It contains an introduction to the play, analysis of scenes and characters, and a commentary on some of the issues raised by the play. Line references are to the Pelican Shakespeare, edited by Alfred Harbage.

When you use this book remember that it is no more than an aid to your study. It will help you find passages quickly and perhaps give you some ideas for essays. But remember: *This book is not a substitute for reading the play and it is your response and your knowledge that matter.* These are the things the examiners are looking for, and they are also the things that will give you the most pleasure. Show your knowledge and appreciation to the examiner, and show them clearly.

Introduction: Background to Henry IV, Part I

Henry IV, Part I is the first of two plays which deal with the troubled reign of Henry Bolingbroke and the eventual succession of his son, Prince Hal, as Henry V. It is, in the broadest sense of the word, a political play. Its main subject is power, who has it and why, and the qualities necessary for using it justly.

These questions of power were of vital interest to Elizabethan audiences. By the 1590s Elizabeth I was an old woman and had no children to succeed her on the throne. This lack of an heir led to a power vacuum which an ambitious noble might hope to fill by using force to make himself king. In an age when elections were unheard of, this situation naturally led people to consider the problems of political power and order in society.

The Elizabethans' concern about their political future was heightened by the fact that they had a frightening example, in the not too distant past, of what could happen to a country when a monarch was weak and the succession uncertain: that example lay in the Wars of the Roses, the civil wars which tore England apart between 1398 and 1485, when the Tudor dynasty was established after Henry VII defeated Richard III.

Shakespeare wrote eight 'history plays' which cover this whole period. The two parts of *Henry IV* come in the middle of a series of four plays which begins with *Richard II* and ends with *Henry V*. In *Richard II* Henry Bolingbroke is exiled, then later returns to depose the weak and unpopular king with the help of the same noblemen who oppose him in *1 Henry IV*. Thus, by deposing the rightful king, he begins the long series of power struggles which constitute the Wars of the Roses.

It is essential, when studying these plays, to bear in mind the Elizabethans' vastly different view of government and monarchy from our own. For them, a king was the 'Lord's anointed'; his right to rule came directly from God and therefore opposition to a king was not only criminal but sinful. As long as all were agreed that a king had a rightful claim to the throne there was a reasonable chance of peace and good government. However, there were several factors which were dangerous for order and stable government.

Firstly, even if he were thought to be the rightful heir, a man might not have the necessary qualities for being a good king; he might be too interested in distracting pleasures and luxury, or just too weak to control a whole nation. Secondly, there might not be general agreement that he was the rightful king. Finally, either or both of these first two factors might encourage the powerful nobles to rebel.

In *Henry IV*, all three are important themes. At the beginning of the play we see a man who has deposed the rightful king and feels guilty because of this. His son and heir, Prince Hal, spends his time in taverns with disreputable companions; he does not seem to be learning any of the skills he will need as king. The kingdom has been invaded from the west by Owen Glendower and from the north by Douglas. The noblemen who helped Henry to the crown are resentful of his power, to which, they feel, he has no more right than they have. It is the development and intertwining of these themes, public and private, that make *Henry IV* such a fascinating play. We move from domestic scenes to great battles, from tavern to court, prince to thief, and in doing so we are given a panoramic view of the nation.

It seems that Shakespeare wrote *I Henry IV* in 1596. We do not know if he originally intended to write a second part, but we can see in the second half of the play that he is preparing us for a sequel (in Act IV Scene iv the Archbishop of York is raising another army; we know the rebellion will not be crushed at Shrewsbury). In his 'history plays' Shakespeare did not follow precisely the historical facts. In this play, for instance, the King is an old man, while Hal and Hotspur are roughly the same age. In reality the King was about as old as Hotspur, and Hal was much younger. Shakespeare altered details and compressed events into a shorter space of time in order to heighten the dramatic impact of the play. It does not affect our enjoyment of the play that Shakespeare has not written a history that sticks closely to the facts; he is using these facts to create a drama which will be both instructive and entertaining.

Synopsis

The King announces that, although the country is war-weary, he will begin a new war abroad. This will be a crusade to the Holy Land which, he hopes, will unite the nation, healing the wounds caused by civil strife. He asks Westmoreland how the preparations are progressing. We learn that the country is still not free of trouble: Mortimer's army has been defeated, and Mortimer himself captured by the Welsh under Glendower. Furthermore, there is news of a battle in the north between Hotspur and the Scots under Douglas. The outcome, says Westmoreland, is still uncertain. Henry, though, is better informed. He reveals that the Scots have been defeated, and many noblemen captured. Westmoreland's praise of the victory urges Henry to reflect sadly on the difference between Hotspur, son of Henry Percy, the powerful Earl of Northumberland, and his own son Hal; the former is 'the theme of honour's tongue', while Hal is a dishonourable ne'er-do-well. Henry returns to the matter in hand; he is angry because Hotspur has refused to give up his prisoners to him. Westmoreland suggests that this shows the influence of Worcester, ill-disposed to Henry in all things. Henry reveals that he has sent for the Percys to explain themselves and that, as a result of these further troubles, the crusade has been postponed.

We now meet Falstaff and Hal (I, ii). Falstaff's character, and the nature of their relationship, is quickly established. From Hal's jokes we learn that Falstaff is a man of gross appetites, untouched by everyday cares and responsibilities. Falstaff, we see, likes to think of himself as a swaggering highwayman. While they pun and joke about robbery, Hal's witticisms take a more serious turn. He subtly distances himself from Falstaff and we see that he is not entirely a part of the tavern world Falstaff inhabits. Poins enters and informs them of the plan for a robbery at Gad's Hill. Falstaff unsuccessfully tries to persuade Hal to join them. Poins asks Falstaff to leave so that he can try to persuade the Prince. This he does by explaining the practical joke he wishes to play: they will rob the robbers. After several objections Hal finally agrees when Poins promises him Falstaff's 'incomprehensible lies' when they meet after the incident. Poins leaves, and Hal, now alone, delivers an important soliloquy. He reveals that he is well aware of the true nature of his companions but that he will keep their company until such time as it suits him to cast them off. This will be when his reformation will appear to most effect, like the sun breaking through thick clouds that have obscured it.

We return to the court (I, iii) where the King appears with his courtiers and the Percys. Henry is angry and has determined to be firmer with his troublesome nobles. Worcester insolently reminds Henry of the part the Percys played in helping him to the throne; Henry's irate response is to expel him from court. Now Hotspur, in a lively and humorous speech, explains why he has not surrendered his Scottish prisoners to the King. His contrast of the ridiculously foppish messenger with himself and his bloodstained soldiers wins the approval of Blunt. Henry, though, is not satisfied; for Hotspur still refuses to yield his prisoners unless the King ransoms Mortimer who, having been defeated by the Welsh, has now married Glendower's daughter. Henry considers Mortimer to be a traitor; Hotspur is outraged and, as proof of Mortimer's loyalty, cites the heroic struggle with Glendower on 'gentle Severn's sedgy bank'. Henry denies the fight ever took place and, commanding Hotspur to send him his prisoners, leaves.

Hotspur is enraged, but is restrained by his father. They are joined by Worcester, to whom they explain the cause of Hotspur's anger. We learn that Mortimer had been proclaimed heir to the throne by Richard I I, and that the Percys had played a part in the former king's deposition.

Worcester and Northumberland complain that, as a result of Richard's murder, they are now 'foully spoken of'. Hotspur's offended honour demands revenge for this and for their loss of favour. Worcester tries to explain to him the plot that has already been laid, but is interrupted by Hotspur's outbursts on the subject of honour and by the declaration of his resolution to overthrow Henry. Eventually Hotspur calms down and Worcester explains his plan: Douglas, Glendower, the Archbishop of York and the Percys will join together against Henry. Worcester says they must either depose Henry or be crushed by him, since he will always see them as a danger to his own safety. The scene ends with Hotspur gleefully anticipating the civil war which will follow.

Act II begins with a complete change in scene and atmosphere. From the intrigue and splendour of the court we move to the yard of an inn at daybreak, where two Carriers are preparing for the day's journey and grumbling about the shortcomings of their accommodation. Gadshill enters and tries to coax from them details of their itinerary, but they are too suspicious to reveal anything. The Carriers leave and Gadshill calls the Chamberlain (an inn servant) who supplies information on the robbers' victims. They joke about the exalted station of their accomplices, and Gadshill then leaves.

Now we go to the scene of the robbery (II, ii). Poins and Hal enter, having hidden Falstaff's horse. This is a cause of great discomfort to Falstaff, who comes in complaining of the trick. He rails against the dishonesty of thieves and bellows for his horse. Now the other thieves enter; the travellers are approaching. The arrangements are made and Falstaff is given his horse, while Poins and Hal go off to prepare their joke. The travellers enter and are robbed, Falstaff urging on his companions with bloodthirsty cries. They leave with their booty and Hal and Poins come back to carry out their plan. Falstaff returns with the others, bemoaning the cowardice of Hal and Poins. At this point these two spring out and rob the robbers; Falstaff and his friends flee, leaving the booty behind. Hal and Poins enjoy their success and prepare to depart.

Once again there is a great contrast in setting as we find Hotspur in his castle, alone (II, iii). He is reading a letter which sets out the writer's reasons for not joining the conspiracy against the King. Although the objections might seem eminently reasonable to us, Hotspur interrupts his reading to rail against the writer's supposed cowardice.

As he resolves to leave that same night, his wife enters. She is worried about her husband and asks, in a touching speech, why he has lately seemed so distraught. Hotspur ignores her and gives directions for his departure. Kate, though, is persistent and questions him again. His joking reply is evasive; she can get nothing out of him. Hotspur tells her she must know nothing, except that he is leaving. But, he says, she will follow him the next day.

In the tavern, Hal is in high spirits (I I, iv). He explains to Poins that he has been drinking with 'a leash of drawers', who think him a fine fellow for his lack of airs. He wants to play a joke on Francis, one of the drawers, to demonstrate the way in which his vocabulary is limited to the needs of his job. With Poins calling to him from off-stage and Hal questioning him on-stage, the bemused Francis can do little but reply 'Anon, anon, sir'. Poins asks, 'What's the issue?' ('What's the point of this joke?'). But there is no point; it simply shows that Hal is 'now of all humours', that he is feeling at his best and most spirited. Hal's mind suddenly turns to Hotspur, whom he parodies as a rough and bloodthirsty murderer.

Falstaff now enters with his cronies. He pretends to be offended by the increasing cowardice in the world and conspicuously ignores Hal. Poins and the Prince eventually persuade him to reveal the reason for his hurt feelings. Falstaff claims his booty has been taken after a heroic struggle with a great many adversaries. His story becomes progressively more absurd, the number of opponents increasing with every minute. At length Hal can take no more; he confronts Falstaff with the truth. Falstaff at once supplies a suitably ridiculous reason for his behaviour and tries to change the subject. He goes out to speak with a nobleman from court who bears a message for Hal. We learn from the other thieves how Falstaff carefully prepared them all for his story ('... to tickle our noses with speargrass to make them bleed, and then to beslubber our garments with it ...').

Falstaff returns with the news that the rebellion is under way and urges Hal to 'practise an answer' to his father. First, Falstaff plays the King with Hal as himself. With ridiculous pomposity he berates Hal for the company he keeps. Only one man is a paragon of virtue –

Falstaff. Hal, outraged, 'deposes' Falstaff and himself plays the King; now we see Falstaff described as a gross and corrupt tempter leading the Prince from the true path. Just as Hal, playing his father, is about to 'banish' Falstaff, a knocking at the door announces the arrival of the Sheriff. The thieves hide while Hal covers up for them and for himself. When the Sheriff leaves, Hal and Poins discover Falstaff 'asleep behind the arras'. In his pocket they find a tavern bill indicating the grossness of his appetites.

Hal, his mood altered by news of the rebellion, decides to return to court. They 'must all to the wars'. Falstaff, 'this fat rogue', will be given command of a company of foot-soldiers. The money from the robbery will, Hal says, be repaid.

The action moves to a meeting of the rebels in Wales, where they are preparing to divide the kingdom (III, i). Here Glendower and Mortimer make their only appearance in the play. Hotspur and Glendower soon start to quarrel because Hotspur refuses to believe Glendower's stories of the supernatural events which accompanied his birth. Glendower repeats his claims and Hotspur his denials until, exasperated by Hotspur's stubborn disbelief, Glendower suggests they look at the map. The rebels have divided England and Wales into three petty kingdoms. On the next day, says Mortimer, they will set out for Shrewsbury. With characteristic delayed reaction Hotspur complains that his share is smaller than the others'. To enlarge it he will change the course of the river Trent. Glendower says he will not, and again they argue childishly until Glendower gives way. Hotspur now says it is an unimportant matter and asks if they shall go. Glendower leaves to bring the ladies while Hotspur, in answer to Mortimer's criticism, reveals how much Glendower's long-winded boasting has annoyed him. Mortimer praises Glendower's achievements, and Worcester takes part and criticizes Hotspur's rudeness and thought-lessness.

Glendower returns with his daughter (now married to Mortimer) and Kate, Hotspur's wife. Glendower translates for his daughter and for Mortimer, who does not understand Welsh, while Hotspur and Kate show their affection for each other through their jokes. With the contrast between Mortimer's reluctance to leave his wife and Hotspur's haste to be off to battle the scene ends.

At the English court an interview takes place between Hal and his father (III, ii). The King wonders if Hal's misbehaviour is a punishment for his own past misdeeds, since he can find no other explanation for the low company Hal keeps. Hal asks his father's pardon, saying that malicious rumour-mongers have invented many stories about him. In a long speech Henry now reviews Hal's shortcomings in the light of his own behaviour when young. He preserved his dignity, Henry says, by maintaining his distance from the common people who were therefore all the more awe-struck when he did appear. Richard II, he says, debased himself and the crown by mixing constantly with fools and commoners. The people became sick of him and lost their sense of the awe and mystery of kingship. Hal's reply is a short but significant one: he will be more what is expected of a prince. Henry continues by saying that as Richard II can be compared with Hal, so Hotspur can now be compared with the young Henry. Hotspur, says Henry, has more right by worth to the throne than Hal, having proved himself to be the greatest and most chivalrous soldier of his time. But why, says Henry, am I telling you of rebellion, since you are as likely to join Hotspur as fight against him? Hal now solemnly swears to redeem himself by defeating Hotspur. The force and sincerity of Hal's words move Henry to an expression of deep relief.

Blunt now enters with the news that the rebel armies have met at Shrewsbury. Henry reveals that Westmoreland and Prince John have already set out; it only remains for himself and Hal to do the same.

Back in the tavern (III, iii) Falstaff is complaining to Bardolph that he is wasting away, an idea which is obviously ridiculous. He also complains that 'villainous company' has corrupted him – another unlikely idea. A slighting remark launches Falstaff on a long flight of fancy about Bardolph's glowing red face. The Hostess enters and Falstaff tackles her over the pickpockets who frequent her inn. He claims he has lost a valuable ring. Just as Falstaff is slandering Hal, the Prince enters, in military style, with Peto. Falstaff explains his loss to Hal while the Hostess tries to tell Hal of Falstaff's slanders. Losing patience with Falstaff's inventions, Hal savagely criticizes him; Falstaff is unabashed. He 'forgives' the Hostess, who withdraws in confusion. We learn that the money from the robbery has been repaid. Hal tells Falstaff he has got him 'a charge of foot' and Falstaff reveals how he hopes to profit from the war. Hal issues instructions for their departure, leaving Falstaff to his breakfast.

The rebels have gathered at Shrewsbury, where Hotspur greets Douglas (I V, i) with high praise. Douglas concedes to Hotspur superiority in honour. A messenger arrives with letters from Northumberland, who is sick and cannot make the journey to join them. Nor, says his letter, will he send his army under another's command. Worcester and Hotspur agree that this is a grave blow, but Hotspur quickly changes his mind; it is an advantage, he believes, to keep something in reserve. Douglas agrees, but Worcester is more worried. He fears Northumberland's absence will be construed as dissension, or fear. Hotspur dismisses this, claiming that their enterprise will be thought all the more honourable for his father's absence. Sir Richard Vernon enters, announcing the approach of the King's forces. Hotspur especially wants to hear news of Hal, and Vernon describes Hal's preparations for battle in terms of the warmest admiration and praise, showing him as a worthy rival in chivalry to Hotspur. Hotspur cannot bear to hear this and interrupts. He sees Hal and his friends as sacrifices to be offered up by himself to the god of war. Vernon then gives them further bad news: Glendower is unable to join them for another fourteen days. Both Douglas and Worcester are disturbed by this, but Hotspur bravely (and rashly) dismisses the disparity between the rebels' and the King's forces.

Falstaff and Bardolph, too, are on the road to Shrewsbury (I V, ii). We see Falstaff send Bardolph for wine, but neglect to give him any money. Alone, Falstaff delivers a monologue in which we learn how he has recruited his wretched band of soldiers. He has allowed those with money to buy themselves out, and has been left with the poorest and weakest. Even he is ashamed of them. Hal and Westmoreland enter. Hal asks whose are the 'pitiful rascals' he has seen. With absurd pride Falstaff replies that they are his, dismissing their condition by saying, callously, that they will serve as cannon-fodder. Hal and Westmoreland leave, urging Falstaff to make haste. He, too, leaves for Shrewsbury, but not without emphasizing his reluctance.

In the rebel camp a heated discussion is taking place over when to give battle (I V.3). Hotspur and Douglas want to fight that same night, while Worcester and Vernon favour the more prudent course of waiting for all their forces to arrive. The argument is threatening to become a brawl after Douglas has accused Vernon of cowardice, when a trumpet sounds a parley and Sir Walter Blunt enters 'with gracious offers from the King'. He is courteously received and, after affirming his loyalty to Henry, sets out the King's offer: Henry wishes to know their reasons for rebellion, offers to right any wrongs he may have done them and promises pardons for all. In reply Hotspur gives his version of Henry's rise to the throne. He tells how his family supported Henry, who had given them his word that he wished to claim nothing more than his own lands and titles. He recounts how Henry took it upon himself to carry out reforms, win the people's affection and, eventually, gain the crown and execute Richard. He now comes to the real grievances: the refusal to ransom Mortimer, the slight to his own honour in demanding the Scottish prisoners and the removal of Henry's favour from the Percys. Blunt asks if this is what he should tell the King but, unusually thoughtful, Hotspur says the rebels will retire to discuss the proposals.

The scene shifts to York where the Archbishop (whom we meet only in this one brief scene) is giving letters to his servant Sir Michael (I V, iv). Fearing the rebels' defeat and a move by the King against himself, he is organizing support for another army to continue the rebellion. We are thus prepared for the King's victory at Shrewsbury – and a sequel to *I Henry IV*.

At sunrise in the King's camp Henry and Hal discuss the rough weather which heralds the day's battle (V, i). Worcester and Vernon enter to bring the rebels' reply to the King's proposals. The King asks Worcester if he will renounce rebellion and become a loyal subject once again. Worcester claims that he has not sought rebellion and recounts the story of Henry's rise to power, emphasizing, like Hotspur, Henry's

ambition and the Percys' help. He complains of Henry's ungratefulness, of how the Percys now fear the fate that befell Richard II. Henry
retorts that these are merely excuses to justify the rebellion and accuses
the conspirators of spreading such stories to stir up discontent. Hal now
intervenes. He is fulsome in his praise of Hotspur and owns to being
'a truant to chivalry' himself. He makes the offer of single combat with
Hotspur 'to save the blood on either side'. Henry agrees to this
solution; he will risk his son because of the love he bears his people.
If Hotspur accepts the challenge, there will be a general pardon.
Worcester and Vernon leave. Hal fears the offer will not be accepted
and the King orders the final preparations for battle to be made.

Falstaff and Hal bid each other farewell. Hal's leave-taking is less
affectionate than Falstaff would have liked. Alone, Falstaff delivers a
monologue on the subject of honour by the end of which he has proved,
to his own satisfaction at least, that honour is an empty idea.

In the rebels' camp Worcester tells Vernon that Hotspur must not
know of the King's 'liberal and kind offer' (V, ii). He attempts to justify
his deceit by saying that the King cannot possibly keep his word.
Hotspur's behaviour will be pardoned because of his youth, and all the
blame will fall on Worcester and Northumberland. Vernon reluctantly
agrees to withhold the truth. Hotspur now enters and is told that the
King will soon call them to join battle. He sends Douglas to free
Westmoreland and convey the rebels' defiance. Worcester says that the
King has no mercy, but he does mention Hal's challenge (without
adding anything about the King's offer). Ironically, Hotspur wishes
that he and Hal might be the only ones to fight that day. He asks how
Hal delivered his challenge. Vernon (as in IV, i) praises Hal's chivalry,
and suggests that, if he survives, he will be a good king. Hotspur
expresses his surprise, and then calls his companions to arms. He
impatiently dismisses a messenger bearing letters, and goes on to
express his belief that life without honour is not worth living. Another
messenger brings news of the King's advance. The rebels embrace, the
trumpets sound, and they leave to do battle.

In the midst of battle Douglas enters to find Blunt, disguised as the
King (V, iii). Douglas has already killed Lord Stafford, who was also

disguised as Henry. He calls on Blunt to surrender. Blunt refuses and is killed in the ensuing fight. Hotspur enters to find Douglas overjoyed at having (he believes) killed the King. Hotspur reveals Blunt's true identity and discloses that many are disguised as Henry. Douglas vows to kill them all, and they both leave.

Falstaff now enters and discovers Blunt's body. He sees Blunt's death as proof that he was a man of honour, but at the same time we learn that Falstaff himself has callously led his own soldiers to a place where they have been massacred. Hal arrives and demands to know why Falstaff is standing idle when so many deaths are unavenged. He asks for a sword. Falstaff claims he has 'paid Percy', but on learning that Hotspur is still alive he elects to keep his sword and offers Hal his pistol. In the holster Hal finds only a bottle of wine. Angrily he throws it at Falstaff and leaves.

The King enters with his sons and Westmoreland (V, iv). He begs Hal to rest and have his wounds dressed. Hal nobly refuses to do so while the outcome of the battle is still uncertain. Prince John and Westmoreland rejoin the fray. Hal and the King speak of the young Prince John's bravery. As Hal leaves, Douglas enters to confront Henry, believing at first that the man before him may be another 'counterfeit' king. They fight and, as Henry is on the point of defeat, Hal returns to save his father's life by putting Douglas to flight. The King tells Hal he has now fully redeemed his 'lost opinion' by showing how much he values his father's life. Hal replies that it was an outrageous slander for anyone to claim that he wished his father dead. Henry leaves to rejoin the battle.

We now reach the climax of the play as Hotspur enters to find Hal. Hal tells him they can no longer 'share in glory' – one or the other must die. Hal says he will defeat Hotspur – 'all the budding honours on thy crest/I'll crop to make a garland for my head'. Enraged by this, Hotspur attacks. As they begin to fight Falstaff enters and bellows encouragement to Hal. He is cut short, however, by the arrival of Douglas, who attacks him. Falstaff falls down as if he were dead, and now attention is focused again on Hal and Hotspur. Hal deals his rival a mortal blow, and in his dying speech Hotspur says he has less thought for the loss of life than the loss of of his honours. Hal speaks movingly over the dead Hotspur and covers his face. He then notices Falstaff lying on the ground and, thinking him dead, bids him farewell. Hal leaves and Falstaff gets to his feet, still justifying his cowardice, in this case because it has saved his skin. Seeing Hotspur it occurs to him that he could claim the honour of having killed him, and he stabs the dead warrior. Hal and his brother enter and are amazed to find Falstaff alive and carrying Hotspur's body on his back. Falstaff says that he expects to be ennobled for having killed Hotspur. He attempts to overcome Hal's disbelief with a vivid story of how he and Hotspur 'fought a long hour by Shrewsbury clock'. Hal, of course, does not believe Falstaff, but assures him that, 'if a lie may do thee grace,/I'll gild it with the happiest terms I have'. A trumpet announces the rebels' defeat. Falstaff, alone, vows that if he is rewarded he will reform and 'live cleanly, as a nobleman should do'.

The King's party enters, with Worcester and Vernon prisoners (V, v). Henry rebukes Worcester for his lies and Worcester admits that he acted only in his own interests. He accepts his fate and Henry orders him and Vernon to be summarily executed. Hal describes how Douglas was captured when trying to escape, having seen his men retreat in disorder. As a sign of his regard for Douglas's bravery Hal orders him to be given his freedom.

The play ends with Henry dividing his forces to confront the remaining rebels in Wales and the north. Thus, although Hotspur has been defeated, the rebellion has not yet been completely crushed.

Scene by Scene Analysis

ACT I SCENE i

Act I opens with a grave and informative scene which contains the seeds of all the themes which will be developed in the course of the play: honour, the nature of kingship, the education of a prince, the evils of rebellion. This first scene also refers back to *Richard II*, at the end of which Henry Bolingbroke deposed the legitimate king and became Henry IV. (Richard was subsequently murdered and the country torn by faction and rivalry.)

Now, at the beginning of *Henry IV*, we see the King as an old and tired man suffering from a guilty conscience. In the very first line of the play his use of the royal 'we' identifies his problems with those of the nation; both are 'shaken' and 'wan with care'. Henry describes the very soil of England as bloodthirsty. The land has been wounded and in the 'furious close of civil butchery', friend has fought against friend, brother against brother. To unite the nation, Henry has decided to lead a crusade to the Holy Land. He asks the Earl of Westmoreland how the Council has decided to further this enterprise. Westmoreland replies that their discussions were interrupted by the news that the Welsh, under 'the irregular and wild Glendower', have captured Mortimer, and therefore the crusade must be postponed. There is yet worse news. Westmoreland tells of a battle in the north between the English, under 'gallant Hotspur', and the Scots, led by 'brave Archibald', the Earl of Douglas. The outcome, he says, is not known. Here the King proves to be better informed. From Sir Walter Blunt he has learnt that Hotspur has won a great victory and taken many prisoners. As Westmoreland says, 'It is a conquest for a prince to boast of' (I, i, 77). This causes Henry to reflect on the contrast between Hotspur, 'the theme of honour's tongue', and his own son Prince Hal, whose reputation is stained by 'riot and dishonour'. He even goes so far as to wish they had been exchanged when infants, so strongly does he feel the difference between them.

From praise of Hotspur, though, Henry turns to criticism. He is angry because Hotspur has refused to yield him all the prisoners except one. Westmorland suggests that it is the influence of Worcester, opposed in everything to the King, which has made Hotspur 'prune himself' (preen himself, like a hawk) and act so defiantly. Henry replies that he has sent for Hotspur to explain himself.

This first scene, then, sketches with great economy the main themes of the play. The language of the opening speech – in which the very soil is described as bloodthirsty, the flowers as bruised – shows how much England has already suffered. We quickly learn that 'frighted peace' will have no time to breathe. Due to foreign invasion and internal division, England is to suffer even more. In addition, Henry has his own personal grief. His son and heir is a dissolute wastrel who seems unlikely to make a worthy successor.

ACT I SCENE ii

From a scene in which King and noblemen consider matters of great political importance, we are transported to a completely different atmosphere. We move from the public to the private world. The tone changes from the serious to the comic and the characters are concerned with personal, rather than political, issues.

Shakespeare has two main dramatic intentions in this scene: to establish the characters of Falstaff and Hal, and to show us what kind of relationship exists between them. Thus most of the scene is given to these two characters, with Poins making an appearance only half-way through.

Falstaff is very quickly fixed in our minds. The scene opens with him asking the time, suggesting that he may just be waking up (or he may have been woken by Hal). This larger-than-life figure, probably unkempt and yawning, is told by the heir to the throne that clock-time is irrelevant to him; Falstaff's appetites are the measure of his time and his principal interests are wine, food and women. After only ten lines of the scene, we have a very clear picture of Falstaff.

The following exchanges between the two might surprise us by the familiarity with which Falstaff treats the heir apparent. He calls the prince 'Hal' and 'sweet wag' and seems to regard him as an equal (compare this with the reverence shown by the Sheriff in I I, iv, who addresses Hal as 'my Lord'). Falstaff replies to Hal's jest about the time by saying that indeed he does not live by day time, for 'we that take purses go by the moon' (Phoebus, here, is the sun-god and Diana goddess of the moon). As the moon governs the tides, so it governs the fortunes of robbers. Hal takes up the theme by reminding Falstaff that the tide might carry him as high as the gallows – the first indication that their relationship is not as close as Falstaff would like to think and that Hal has a clear idea of Falstaff's moral corruption.

Falstaff changes the subject, but his sally about the Hostess of the tavern goes too far. Hal quickly puts Falstaff in his place by reminding him that he might end up in a 'buff jerkin' – prison clothes. He also reminds us that he has kept his distance from the inhabitants of the tavern-world and that his reputation is not too tarnished by association with them. Falstaff asks Hal not to 'hang a thief' when he is King. I shall not, says Hal, but *you* will. Falstaff takes that to mean he will be a judge (an absurd idea which he seems to take seriously) but Hal corrects him: he will be a hangman. All this talk of prisons and gallows has made Falstaff 'melancholy'. He goes on to tell Hal that a 'Lord of the Council' has scolded him about Hal's behaviour. They swap parodies of religious language and Falstaff sanctimoniously says he will mend his ways, claiming, in a complete reversal of the truth, that Hal has corrupted him. Hal sees through Falstaff's 'repentance' and traps him by asking where they shall 'take a purse tomorrow'. Falstaff immediately forgets his religious mood and happily replies that he will take part in a robbery.

Here Poins enters. After greeting Falstaff abusively and exchanging witticisms with Hal, he reveals the plans for the robbery to be carried out at Gad's Hill. Pilgrims and rich merchants are to be the victims. Falstaff asks Hal if he will join them. Hal teases him; first he says no, then yes, then again no. Hal's initial reply – 'Who, I rob? I a thief?' – shows us that the idea of robbery is extremely distasteful to him.

Poins asks Falstaff to leave so that he can persuade Hal to join them. After Falstaff's exit Poins explains to Hal the practical joke he intends to play. Hal is at first unenthusiastic, raising objections to the plan, but Poins persuades him by the promise of the 'incomprehensible lies' Falstaff will later tell. Hal agrees to go and Poins exits to make the preparations, leaving Hal alone. Hal's important soliloquy here shows us to what extent he is aware of the nature of his tavern companions. He says he knows what they are like, but will put up with their 'idleness' for a while. He will imitate the sun (a common image of royalty) by allowing himself to be covered with clouds, so that when he reappears 'he may be more wonder'd at'. Holidays are welcome only if they are infrequent; so only 'rare accidents' (unexpected events) will impress people. When he gives up his 'loose behaviour' he will, like shining metal on a dull background, be all the more appreciated. He will make up for his misspent time when his reform is least expected.

This speech indicates that Hal knows what he is doing. Up to this point we have noticed that Hal maintains a distance in his relationship with Falstaff. Hal knows that, sooner or later, he will have to break with him and his friends. For the time being, though, he can have it both ways; he can enjoy himself in this irresponsible company, secure in the knowledge that he has the strength to change when the times require it. We, too, now understand that he is not dissolute and corrupt, that he will become a real prince. We can watch the development of his character, sure that he will rise to the challenge presented by the rebels.

ACT I SCENE iii

This scene returns us to the court and the world of power-politics. Northumberland, Worcester and Hotspur have arrived to give their reasons for refusing the King their prisoners. Henry enters and is obviously angry. He says that he has been too mild and forgiving and, as a result, the Percys have taken advantage of him. Now he will be more of a king – 'Mighty and to be feared'. Worcester says they do not deserve this, especially as the Percys helped Henry to the crown. Enraged by what he considers to be insolence, Henry expels Worcester from the court. He turns to Northumberland and Hotspur for an explanation of their refusal to give up the prisoners.

In a long speech (I, iii, 29–69) Hotspur gives a lively and colourful account of how, at the battle's conclusion, a 'popingay' (a ridiculously affected young man) demanded his prisoners for the King. Hotspur humorously contrasts this courtier with himself and his soldiers. The former is 'perfumèd like a milliner', 'neat, trimly dressed', and sniffs a scented pouncet box to take away the smell of battle. Hotspur and his men, however, are dirty and bloody after their heroic deeds. During this speech, full of vivid imagery, we can imagine Hotspur acting out the part of the 'popingay', mimicking his voice and gestures, and effectively making his point. He was, he says, so angry that he cannot now remember what he said. Blunt comments that the circumstances excuse his behaviour, if he will now take back his words. Henry, though, is not so easily appeased. He points out that Hotspur will not give up his prisoners unless he, Henry, ransoms Mortimer (Hotspur's brother-in-law) who, having been captured by the Welsh, has married the daughter of his captor, Glendower. Why, says Henry, should he pay to 'redeem a traitor home'? Let him starve on the Welsh mountains.

This is too much for Hotspur. In anger and disbelief he repeats the last words of Henry's speech: 'Revolted Mortimer?' To prove Mortimer's loyalty he gives a lengthy and ornate description of a heroic fight between Mortimer and Glendower. As always when describing a battle, Hotspur is carried away by his excitement. His speech, while containing some images of great beauty, is ranting and rhetorical.

His bombastic justification of Mortimer is punctured by Henry's reply. He says the fight never, in fact, took place. He commands them to deliver up their prisoners and leaves.

Hotspur is beside himself with rage; he wants to express his feelings, even at the risk of his own safety, and attempts to follow the King. He is restrained by his father, but continues to rant. Worcester returns and Hotspur explains the cause of his rage, saying that Henry trembled 'even at the name of Mortimer'. Worcester is not surprised. Mortimer had been named heir to the throne by Richard II, and might therefore be considered dangerous by Henry IV.

We learn from Worcester and Northumberland that they played an important part in helping Henry to seize the crown, for which they are now criticized and 'foully spoken of'. Hotspur is scandalized that they should have sacrificed their good name to replace Richard II with Henry. He says they must recover their 'banished honours' and revenge themselves on this 'proud King' who is plotting to kill them. We notice here that Hotspur's anger springs more from the idea that Henry has been ungrateful to the Percys than from any notion of real justice and honour. Again he is carried away by his rhetoric and his 'imagination of some great exploit'. Instead of listening to his uncle he constantly interrupts him. He childishly wants to keep all the honour in the world for himself. Mention of the prisoners leads to several more outbursts until eventually, at line 254, he has said enough and is ready to listen to his calmer, and more astute, uncle.

Worcester now explains the plot against Henry. The prisoners will be used to forge an alliance with the Scots. He will persuade the Archbishop of York, angry because of his brother's execution, to join them. Then all will join with Glendower and Mortimer in Wales.

Worcester's reason for rebellion is that Henry 'will always think him in our debt,/And think we think ourselves unsatisfied' until he has removed them. This is more of an excuse than a valid reason; as we see later, when the rebels divide the kingdom in three, they are all interested in expanding their own power and do not wish to acknowledge any sovereign authority but their own.

At the beginning of this scene we were presented with a king who is very different from the tired man we saw in Act I Scene i. He is now firmer and more resolute; he is not prepared to brook any challenge to his authority. This new attitude does not, we notice, cause the Percys' rebellion – Worcester has already laid his plans and Henry's renewed authority merely helps Worcester to sell his reasons to Hotspur. The rebels are prompted to their action by ambition and resentment of a power that they helped to promote. They have no thought of what is best for the nation, but only of their personal good. This outlook is exemplified by Hotspur, who is so obsessed by his narrow idea of honour that he is prepared to plunge England into civil war for the sake of his pride and glory. Worcester and Northumberland, cold and calculating politicians, do not even have the noble excuse of honour. Their actions seem to be motivated by envy and resentment; if we put Henry on the throne, they reason, why should we not depose him and take his place ourselves?

ACT II SCENE i

This scene takes place in the early morning gloom of the courtyard of an inn. In stark contrast to the last scene of Act I we are in the world of day-to-day cares and concerns. The two Carriers are preparing for their journey to London, and while they call for the ostler to attend to their horses they discuss in rough and lively terms the defects of the accommodation. The food is 'as dank here as a dog', the rooms are infested with fleas and they have to urinate in the fireplace because there is not even a chamber-pot.

We now see a different side of the world of the common people. Unlike Falstaff and his friends, the two Carriers have their own responsibilities and cares in trying to make an honest living; the atmosphere of their tavern is very different from that of Falstaff's.

Gadshill enters and attempts to prise some information out of them, but they are suspicious and tell him nothing. They leave to call the 'gentlemen' who will accompany them on the road.

The Chamberlain (a bedroom attendant) and Gadshill then discuss the robbers and their victims. Gadshill seems to think Falstaff and his companions are a cut above the usual kind of thief, an opinion Falstaff himself would share.

ACT II SCENE ii

Hal and Poins enter. They have hidden Falstaff's horse, and now conceal themselves to enjoy the joke. Given his size, Falstaff's worry is understandable. Alone on stage, he delivers a monologue about how he is 'bewitched' by Poins – he cannot do without his company. He bemoans the problems he will have without a horse. Hal enters and tells him to lie down and listen for the footsteps of their approaching victims. Falstaff replies with a jest at his own expense, asking if they have any levers to lift him up again. The remaining thieves enter, and the pace of the scene quickens. Rapid instructions and quips are exchanged as they prepare for the robbery. Hal and Poins leave to get ready for their practical joke.

In the half-light of early morning the travellers enter and are terrified by the thieves' cries. Falstaff roars bloodthirsty threats, but we can imagine him taking little part in the robbery and, rather, encouraging his friends from the sidelines. The Prince and Poins re-enter and, just as Falstaff is complaining of their cowardice, rob the robbers. Falstaff and his companions flee in terror, leaving their booty.

The comedy of this scene springs from the incongruity of Falstaff's murderous bluster towards the travellers and his cowardice when robbed by Poins and Hal. The sight of Falstaff running, after what he has earlier told us about his helplessness without a horse, adds to the humour. The scene has its serious side; Falstaff's behaviour prepares us for his more serious cowardice later in the play, at the Battle of Shrewsbury.

ACT II SCENE iii

Again there is a swift change of location. We are now at Hotspur's castle in Northumberland, where the scene opens with Hotspur reading a letter from a nobleman who, for very prudent reasons, has refused to join the conspiracy. The reading of the letter is interrupted three times by Hotspur's scornful outbursts. We learn that the conspiracy is gathering momentum and that some of the rebel forces are already on their way to the meeting place. Hotspur distrusts the writer's reluctance to join him; he can only see fear in such reservations. He calls the writer a 'lackbrain' and a 'frosty-spirited rogue', and suspects that he will probably reveal all to the King. Typically intemperate and unreflective, Hotspur dismisses the writer and the discovery of the plot; he will go ahead regardless.

His wife, Kate, enters and the rest of the scene continues in a slightly comical, domestic manner, revealing a tender side of Hotspur we have not seen until now and do not see much of again. She asks why, for the past two weeks, he has been so distant and preoccupied, why he has murmured of war and weapons in his sleep. She wants to know what 'heavy business' has caused such disturbances. Hotspur ignores her questions and gives orders for his departure. When his wife returns to the subject he pretends to misunderstand her. She continues to try to get some information out of him but he teasingly evades her, saying that this is a world for battles, not for love. When he says he does not love her, Kate seems genuinely upset and unsure whether he is joking or not. But, says Hotspur, when he is on his horse *then* he will swear he loves her. He reassures her, saying, 'Whither I go, there shall you go too'.

This view of Hotspur with his wife allows us to see that he is not completely rash and unthoughtful. His troubled sleep shows he is aware, even if only at a subconscious level, of the danger of the conspiracy. His exchanges with his wife reveal a tender and affectionate aspect of his character – an aspect that he represses in his pursuit of honour and power.

ACT II SCENE iv

We move to the tavern for this long and very important scene. It is one of the funniest, and at the same time one of the most revealing, in the play. Having played their practical joke, Poins and the Prince now hope to get their reward – Falstaff's 'incomprehensible lies'. In this they are not disappointed. But there is much more to the scene than this. We now have a further exploration of the relationship between Hal and Falstaff, especially when they exchange the parts of king and prince in an impromptu piece of play-acting. As the political events of the play are now moving forward more quickly we see, too, how they intrude on the irresponsible tavern-world of Falstaff and his friends.

The scene begins with Hal telling Poins of his new friendship with the 'drawers' (the serving-boys) of the inn. He has been drinking with them and they have taken him to their hearts; he is a 'lad of mettle, a good boy' who has none of Falstaff's pride. We are shown that Hal's time spent in the tavern is not time wasted. Indeed, it is an essential part of his education for kingship. For here he learns the 'common touch', the necessary sympathy for the lower orders of society. Not that he regards these 'drawers' as his equals – the joke he plays on Francis, whose response is limited to 'Anon, anon, sir!', shows as much. With Hal on-stage talking to him and Poins calling from a room elsewhere, Francis can do little but repeat his 'Anon, anon, sir!' in bewilderment. In the end Hal is talking gibberish to him, and Francis is scolded by his master for not attending to the guests. It is difficult for us to find the interchange very funny. We might ask with Poins, 'What's the issue?' ('What's the point of it?'). But there does not seem to be one; Hal is simply in high spirits, 'all humours'.

Hal suddenly changes the subject and gives a caricature of Hotspur, whom he sees as a kind of homicidal maniac who cannot have enough of blood and death. (In Act V we shall see that Hal's view of Hotspur is really more generous than this.)

Falstaff enters with his companions. He laments the lack of courage in the world, suggesting that he is one of the few virtuous and brave men left alive. Falstaff here assumes a sanctimonious air which is doubly funny as both the audience and Hal know the truth about what happened at Gad's Hill. Eventually Hal coaxes out of Falstaff the reason for his resentment, and the ludicrous story emerges. We cannot help but admire Falstaff's lying – it is a masterpiece of the tall story. The detail and energy with which he tells it almost seem to convince him of its truth. He is so carried away that he does not notice the multiplication of his assailants: how two become four, seven, eleven. Of course Falstaff comes out of the tale very well; he portrays himself as a heroic knight struggling against overwhelming odds. Hal at last stops him, saying that Falstaff, like his lies, is 'gross as a mountain'. Calmly, he explains what really happened at Gad's Hill. We can imagine Falstaff dumbfounded and a long, long pause after Poins asks him what 'trick' he will employ to explain himself. Falstaff's reply is a brilliant piece of off-the-cuff lying; of course he knew who they were, but was it for him to kill the heir apparent? He rapidly changes the subject and suggests 'a play extempore'. Before this can get under way, however, the Hostess enters to say that a messenger from the King is at the door. Hal sends Falstaff to inquire what news the messenger brings and, while he is absent, the prince learns from Bardolph and Peto the lengths to which Falstaff had gone to lend his story credibility; he had told them to break their swords and bloody their noses and clothes.

Falstaff returns. Despite the gravity of the news, he delivers it in typical joking fashion. Worcester has secretly left the court, the rebels are gathering and Hal must go to his father. Falstaff says that the King will scold Hal, and he begs him to 'practise an answer'. Hal agrees and asks Falstaff to play his father. With a cushion for a crown, his dagger for a sceptre and mounted on a tavern chair for a throne, Falstaff prepares to play the King. He says he will speak in 'King Cambyses' vein'; that is, in the bombastic, ranting style of a play popular in Shakespeare's time. Thus not only his appearance and stage props but also his language mock the dignity and authority of kingship.

Speaking as the King, Falstaff completely distorts the truth. He warns Hal of the company he keeps and how it can, like pitch, stain his reputation. But, he says, there is one 'virtuous man' among his friends – none other than Falstaff. All the gross physical characteristics of Falstaff are turned into virtues – he is a 'goodly portly man' with 'a most noble carriage'. Morally, too, he is above reproach. Stay with him, says Falstaff-as-King, but banish the others.

As with his ridiculous tale of the robbery, Falstaff seems almost to believe what he is saying. For Hal, though, it is too much. After witnessing Falstaff's cowardice and listening to his lies he cannot take this twisted version of the truth. He 'deposes' Falstaff. Hal now plays the King and Falstaff pretends to be Hal.

Hal-as-King compares Falstaff with the devil, leading the Prince away from virtue. Falstaff is a 'bolting hutch of beastliness', a gross, corrupt figure who is nothing but the sum of his appetites and interests. Falstaff-as-Hal counters this harsh judgement by asking if it is a sin to be old and merry, and claims that Falstaff is no corrupter. The picture he paints is sentimental and full of self-deception, yet it is still a touching one. The play-acting ends with Hal-as-King firmly stating that he will banish 'plump Jack'.

This section of Scene iv is a complex one which we must consider carefully. When Hal as the King delivers his savage judgement of Falstaff there are three different perspectives to be considered. Firstly, this must be the opinion of Falstaff Hal believes his father to hold. Secondly, it must, at least in part, be what Hal himself thinks of Falstaff. Finally, it is the way in which Hal will have to view Falstaff when he himself becomes king.

It is clear, then, that by now Hal has completely seen through Falstaff. He knows he will have to break with him when he becomes king. Falstaff does not realize that their relationship must end, nor does he understand how others can see him in such a different light from that in which he views himself.

The arrival of the Sheriff interrupts the role-playing at its most dramatic moment. The robbers hide and Hal remains to talk to the Sheriff, who is accompanied by one of the Carriers from the Gad's Hill robbery. Assuming a more princely manner, Hal denies that any of the suspected men are in the tavern. The Sheriff leaves.

The scene ends on a more relaxed note after the dramatic tension and high spirits of Falstaff's story and the play-acting. Hal and Peto discover Falstaff 'asleep behind the arras, and snorting like a horse'. In his pocket they find a tavern bill which reveals the gargantuan nature of his thirst – gallons of wine, but only a halfpennyworth of bread. Hal, having earlier received the message from his father, says he will set off for the court in the morning, for 'we must all to the wars'. He realizes he must now do his duty. He will obtain for Falstaff 'a charge of foot', even though he knows it will not be to Falstaff's liking. The stolen money will be repaid, he says, with interest.

By the end of Act II, then, the speed of the play is picking up. All the main wheels of the plot have been set in motion. The world of political events and the world of private irresponsibility now begin to converge.

ACT III SCENE i

From the tavern the scene shifts to Wales, where the rebels are meeting to divide the kingdom. We are introduced to two more important rebel leaders – Mortimer and Glendower. As the scene opens Mortimer's words give us an idea of the rebels' over-confidence, the pride that comes before their fall. Hotspur invites the others to sit round the map – which he suddenly realizes he has forgotten. Glendower, though, has it, and they take their positions. Hotspur and Glendower exchange compliments on their fearsome reputations, but Hotspur's compliments quickly turn to insults. Glendower tells of disturbances of a heavenly and earthly nature at his birth; Hotspur retorts that the same disturbances would have occurred if Glendower's mother's cat had had kittens. Glendower repeats himself and Hotspur again contradicts him, saying that he, Hotspur, is not afraid of Glendower. Once more Glendower begins to describe the burning sky and shaking earth, but Hotspur interrupts him with a more down-to-earth explanation of such disturbances. Glendower tells Hotspur that few men could contradict him and get away with it. He presents the strange occurrences that coincided with his birth as evidence of his extraordinary nature. There is no man, he says, who can teach him anything, or who can compare with him in his knowledge of magic. Hotspur replies that 'no man speaks better Welsh' (talks nonsense and brags). Despite Mortimer's attempt to calm Hotspur, they continue bickering. Glendower claims he can 'call spirits from the vasty deep'. So can I, says Hotspur, but will they come? I can teach you to command the devil, says Glendower. And I can teach *you* to shame the devil by telling the truth, says Hotspur. Pleased with himself, he repeats this several times. They persist in their argument until Glendower, realizing he is getting nowhere with Hotspur, suggests they return to the question of the division of the kingdom.

From this childish exchange we begin to understand Glendower and we gain further insight into Hotspur's character. Although undoubtedly brave, Glendower is boastful and long-winded. Hotspur, though, is sharp with him for other reasons than these; he cannot bear to think that someone else could share glory and honour with him (as we have seen in I, iii, 201–8). We now watch the rebels sharing out the kingdom; instead of one strong nation, there will be three petty monarchies. The silly argument between Hotspur and Glendower does not give much hope for future peace. Hotspur is not satisfied with his 'moiety' (share). He complains that a bend in the river Trent cuts out a section of the best land. He will dam it up, so that the land will be in his portion. Again, the rivalry between Glendower and Hotspur erupts. From the distribution of land, the argument turns to the virtue of poetry. Glendower suddenly gives in to Hotspur, who says he does not care any longer – he was only determined to protect his rights.

Such absurd disputes should make us realize the danger the rebels pose to the well-being of society. If they can become so angry before they have even won a battle, what will their rule be like if they do overthrow the King?

Glendower leaves to fetch the women. Hotspur excuses his behaviour by complaining of Glendower's endless magical mumbo-jumbo ('skimble-skamble stuff'). Mortimer, though, praises Glendower's restraint and begs Hotspur to be more temperate in future. Worcester, too, adds his own criticism, a very acute one. He says Hotspur is too 'wilful-blame' (self-willed and rash). This, he says, detracts from Hotspur's praiseworthy qualities and is the root of many of his faults. It is an assessment we probably share.

Glendower returns with the wives of Mortimer and Hotspur. There is a touching contrast between the ways in which the two couples show their affection. Mortimer and his wife do not understand each other's language, so their tender feelings are conveyed by looks and touch. Hotspur and Kate, on the other hand, have a more robust kind of relationship. Their love is expressed through jokes and high spirits. After some music has been played, the scene ends with Hotspur, despite his love for Kate, eager to be away, while Mortimer seems reluctant to part with his new bride.

ACT III SCENE ii

In this scene we see father and son, King and Prince, together for the first time. The King dismisses his attendant lords, leaving Hal alone with him for almost the entire scene.

The King says that Hal must have been sent by God to punish his own 'mistreadings' (he is referring to his deposition of Richard II). Why else should Hal, in spite of his royal blood, be so attached to vulgar pleasures and companions?

Hal, in subdued and repentant mood, replies that he is not guilty of everything he is charged with. He says he will prove untrue many stories that have arisen from malicious gossip; and, in doing so, he will ask his father's pardon for those offences which have been committed out of youthful inexperience.

'God pardon thee!' says Henry. But he is not yet ready to add *his* pardon. He wonders at Hal's pursuits, so unusual in one of his blood. He points out that Hal has lost his place in the Council, is a stranger to the court, and is thought by all to be heading for disaster. The rest of this long speech of Henry's is taken up by a lesson in public relations. Hal's wild indiscretions prompt him to recall his own younger days. He recounts the contrast between himself and Richard II, and how his own discreet and regal behaviour won him the affection of the people. If, he says, he had been so 'lavish' with his presence then as Hal is now, public opinion, which helped him to the throne, would have remained loyal to Richard. By being sparing of his public appearances he maintained his mystery, and was thus all the more 'wondered at', like a comet, when he was seen; remaining aloof, he won the people's affection. Richard, on the other hand, courted popularity in a humiliating fashion, mixing constantly with the common people. He enslaved himself to popularity. By being seen so often the people grew sick of him – they 'surfeited with honey'. Rather than preserving that 'Sun-like majesty' which dazzles when revealed, Richard II had lost all mystery and awe. This, says the King, is the very same danger that Hal is now courting.

Hal's reply – 'I shall hereafter . . ./Be more myself' – has great implications for his development in the rest of the play. To be himself means to be more princely; to reach the maturity and assume the responsibilities which go with his birth and future. The simplicity and sincerity of his language emphasize the change from the Hal of the tavern. Falstaff's joking and high-spirited companion is not visible here; we see the return of a prodigal son, solemnly determined to mend his ways.

Henry, though, has not yet finished. After comparing Hal with Richard II he draws another parallel, this time between Hotspur and himself when he returned from exile to usurp the throne. Hotspur has, he says, more right to the crown than Hal. Is Hotspur not the epitome of honour, brave and successful, acknowledged throughout the Christian world as holding 'military title capital'? Three times he has defeated 'great Douglas' and now he leads a rebellion. But why, he asks, do I tell you this? For you are 'my nearest and dearest enemy'. So appalled and hurt is Henry by Hal's behaviour that he even believes him capable of fighting against him under Hotspur's command.

Hal is obviously hurt by the extent to which he has lost his father's affection and respect. He begs him not to believe he is capable of treason. In a passionate speech Hal swears he will redeem himself. The blood of battle shall wash away his shame. This will be when he and Hotspur meet, face to face. Then, by defeating him, Hal will gain all the honour that Hotspur has amassed. All this Hal solemnly swears to do, or die in the attempt.

The King is greatly moved by this sincere repentance. He tells Hal he will give him his trust and an important command in the war.

The intensity is relaxed as Blunt enters with the news that the rebels have met at Shrewsbury, forming a great and powerful army. The scene ends with Henry informing Hal, and us, of his own preparations for the ensuing struggle.

This central scene of the play is important for another reason besides that of the reconciliation of Hal with the King. Here we are made aware of the essential part that the rivalry between Hal and Hotspur plays in *1 Henry IV*. In the very first scene of the play we noticed how Henry compares the two, to Hal's disadvantage; Hotspur is everything he would like his own son to be. Hal and Hotspur are each conscious of the other's pursuits; in Act I Scene iii Hotspur calls Hal 'that same sword-and-buckler Prince of Wales'; while in Act II Scene iv Hal characterizes Hotspur as a murderous hothead. Neither judgement reveals the respect they feel for each other. Now we see that their rivalry is to be crucial to the salvation, not only of Hal's character, but of the kingdom. The personal and political threads of the play are again entwined, and we are prepared for the climax – the single combat of Hal and Hotspur in Act V.

ACT III SCENE iii

Once more a change of scene brings a great change in atmosphere. We are again in the tavern, where Falstaff is in self-pitying mood. Ridiculously, he asks Bardolph if he thinks he has lost weight ('Do I not dwindle?'). He claims to have once been 'virtuous', but he qualifies this claim to such an extent that his virtue can only have been corruption. Bardolph's jests about his size lead Falstaff to hit back with a series of jokes about Bardolph's glowing red nose and face (which are, like Falstaff's obesity, physical signs of moral corruption). His witticisms and biblical references show us that Falstaff has some learning (now corrupted to suit his own purposes) and that he is, socially and intellectually, the superior of his tavern companions.

The Hostess enters and Falstaff asks her who has picked his pocket. She is affronted by the suggestion that she keeps thieves in her house, even as she is talking to one. We learn that Falstaff owes her money for clothes and for his board and lodging. Falstaff outfaces her by claiming he has lost an expensive ring. When the Hostess replies that Hal has said the ring was only copper, he calls Hal a cowardly rascal whom he, Falstaff, would beat like a dog if he were present. At this moment Hal enters; Falstaff's attitude quickly changes to one of fawning servility. He complains to Hal of his loss (which now includes 'bonds of forty pound apiece'). Hal dismisses it as a mere trifle and the Hostess repeats to him Falstaff's earlier threat to beat him. Falstaff tries to change the subject by insulting the Hostess, but she counters by telling Hal that Falstaff claims he is owed 'a thousand pound' by the Prince. Hal turns on Falstaff – while he is genuinely disgusted, he has not yet reached the point where Falstaff has ceased to be amusing. When Hal asks, 'Art thou not ashamed?', the audacity of Falstaff's reason why he is not is almost admirable. Indeed, to ask Falstaff if he is ashamed seems pointless; to feel shame one must have a sense of right and wrong, which Falstaff almost entirely lacks.

Falstaff turns to the Hostess and, absurdly, 'forgives' her. The honest but stupid woman is bemused by the clever but dishonest Falstaff and she leaves without another word.

Hal tells Falstaff that the problem of the robbery has been cleared up. The money has been repaid: news which Falstaff is unhappy to hear. Falstaff is equally unhappy to hear that Hal has got him command of a company of infantry. 'I would it had been of horse,' he says, not relishing the prospect of walking which, as we have seen, is not one of Falstaff's favourite pastimes. Falstaff's further observations on the war reveal an immensely irresponsible and self-interested attitude; he wonders where he can find a 'fine thief' to make the most of the opportunities for robbery that war presents. The rebels, he says, 'offend none but the virtuous' (and, therefore, do not offend Falstaff). He shows that he has no conception of any more important issue than the gratification of his own desire.

Hal does not reply to these comments – he is concerned with the business of war.

With this scene we leave the tavern for good. From now on Falstaff will be seen in the real world, where actions have significant consequences and moral repercussions. The play now moves on rapidly to its climax, with the shorter scenes of Acts I V and V giving us the impression of movement and purpose.

ACT IV SCENE i

In the rebel camp at Shrewsbury Hotspur greets Douglas with praise of his courage. Douglas returns the compliment, calling Hotspur 'the king of honour'. A messenger enters with letters from Hotspur's father, Northumberland, who is sick. How has he the leisure to be sick, Hotspur wonders, at such a time, and asks who is in command of his troops. The messenger replies that this news is in the letters he has brought.

Hotspur exclaims that Northumberland's sickness infects the whole enterprise – ''Tis catching hither, even to our camp'. He reads the letter, in which Northumberland gives rather unconvincing reasons for not sending his forces under another's command. Worcester remarks that Northumberland's sickness is a great blow. Hotspur begins to agree, and then, typically, breaks off in mid sentence. It is not wise, he says, to place all one's money on a single bet. This way, they will keep something in reserve. Douglas agrees, but Worcester is more concerned. Their enterprise, he says, 'brooks no division'; some will say that Northumberland has stayed away out of prudence. Thus, the rebels will be thought disunited (which they are, as we have seen in Act I I I Scene i), or even afraid.

Not so, replies Hotspur. His father's absence will make their business seem all the more heroic and daring (thus adding to his own honour, we should notice).

Another rebel, Sir Richard Vernon, enters with the news that

Westmoreland and Prince John are approaching. The King, too, has set out for Shrewsbury. Hotspur is anxious to hear news of the 'madcap Prince of Wales' and his companions. In a speech rich in imagery and full of the spirit of medieval chivalry, Vernon describes Hal and his comrades 'as full of spirit as the month of May', and Hal himself plumed, glittering and energetic in his youthful warlike vigour.

Hotspur cries out to him to say no more, unable to bear such fulsome praise of his rival. His thoughts immediately turn to battle and blood; Hal and his companions are sacrifices which Hotspur will offer up, 'all hot and bleeding', to Mars, the god of war. With characteristic impatience he can hardly wait for the battle, when 'Harry to Harry shall, hot horse to horse,/Meet and ne'er part till one drop down a corse'. His mind leaps to Glendower, and Vernon tells him that the Welshman cannot have his army ready for another two weeks. Even the fearless Douglas agrees with Worcester that this is terrible news. Hotspur's isolation is thus increased, but so too is his heroism. Despite his many faults we see him more sympathetically, even with a certain admiration, in this second half of the play.

He valiantly but rashly dismisses the disparity between the rebels' and the King's forces. He leaves to prepare for battle, his last words in the scene – 'Die all, die merrily' – reminding us that his attitude to the value of life is, in quite a different way, as irresponsible as Falstaff's.

ACT IV SCENE ii

Far from the tavern now, Falstaff and Bardolph are marching towards Shrewsbury. They have, however, brought the habits of the tavern with them. Falstaff sends Bardolph ahead to buy wine (for which he neglects to give him money), and we realize that Falstaff is not going to change his ways merely because there is a war on.

Left alone, Falstaff delivers a long monologue in which we learn how he recruited his soldiers. It is a speech which would probably disgust us if Falstaff had not, in spite of his gross faults, established a bond of affection between himself and the audience. This he has achieved partly by the nature of his monologues. Unlike Hal in his soliloquy at the end of I, ii, Falstaff is not really thinking aloud when he is alone on stage. He speaks across the barrier of the stage, acknowledging the presence of an audience. Thus he takes us into his confidence and makes us feel that we, too, might be guilty of the same faults.

He begins his speech with an admission we might never have expected to hear from Falstaff: he is ashamed of his soldiers. As a captain he has the power to conscript men, and his duty in such desperate times is, of course, to find those who will fight best for the King. Falstaff, though, is not concerned with duty, but with his own immediate interests. He has conscripted those men most reluctant and ill-suited to fight – 'toasts-and-butter', with comfortable lives and something to stay at home for. Then he has taken bribes from them to release them. In their place he has conscripted the poorest half-starved weaklings, who have nothing to keep them at home nor any money to buy themselves out. He describes their wretched appearance so vividly that we can understand how even the shameless Falstaff might blush.

Hal and Westmoreland enter and Falstaff, in an attempt to forestall criticism of his slow progress, asks them why they have not yet reached Shrewsbury. Hal asks whose the soldiers are and Falstaff replies, with absurd pride, that they are his. Hal says he has never seen 'such pitiful rascals'. Falstaff's comment shows a terrible cynicism and heartlessness – they will do for cannon-fodder, he says. Hal, eager to be at Shrewsbury, tells Falstaff to make haste and leaves without a farewell. The scene ends with Falstaff revealing that he has been purposely slow; last at a fight, first at a good dinner, he says.

ACT IV SCENE iii

We return to the rebel camp where a heated argument is taking place over when the battle should commence. The impulsive and reckless

Hotspur, with Douglas, would like to fight that very night, while the more reflective Vernon and Worcester want to wait until their forces have arrived. The rapid interchange leads to an argument between Douglas and Vernon about whether the latter is afraid – 'You speak it out of fear and cold heart,' Douglas says. The tensions and personal rivalries within the rebel camp are becoming evident.

The argument, however, is interrupted by the sound of trumpets heralding the arrival of Sir Walter Blunt with messages from the King. Hotspur praises Blunt's reputation and wishes he were on the rebels' side. It could not be, says Blunt, while they 'stand against anointed majesty'. He delivers his message, which is a generous offer of peace and pardon if they can show the King that he has been unjust to them. Hotspur's long reply consists mainly of an account of Henry's rise to power – a rather different one from that told by Henry to Hal in Act III Scene ii. In Hotspur's version, Henry had returned from exile claiming only to seek his inheritance as Duke of Lancaster, and on this basis he was given Northumberland's support. Ambition, though, raised him 'a little higher than his vow'; Henry began to reform injustices and, by doing so, gained great popularity. With Richard II absent in Ireland, Henry executed his representatives in England. Blunt begins to show impatience, and at last Hotspur gets to the point. Henry deposed the King and 'deprived him of his life' – but even this does not appear to be the true source of his grievance. His anger rises when he remembers how Henry allowed Mortimer to remain unransomed in Wales, 'disgraced me in my happy victories', and dismissed his father and uncle from court and Council. He does not substantiate his claim that Henry 'broke oath on oath, committed wrong on wrong'; his rebellion springs from the slight his pride has suffered by Henry demanding his prisoners.

Blunt asks if this is the answer he should return to the King. Hotspur here manages to control his impetuousness and says they will take some time to consider it. They will deliver their answer in the morning.

ACT IV SCENE iv

This brief scene begins with the Archbishop of York giving a servant letters to be delivered to other conspirators against the King. The Archbishop fears that Hotspur's forces will be too weak to defeat the King's. In expectation of defeat at Shrewsbury and of the King then turning his attentions to himself, the Archbishop is trying to raise another army.

This scene serves two purposes. It emphasizes the hopelessness of Hotspur's cause — we can have no doubt now that the rebels will be defeated — and it prepares us for a sequel to the play; by showing the Archbishop here organizing another army we are given to realize that the rebellion will not be crushed, once and for all, at Shrewsbury.

ACT V SCENE i

The King enters, with Hal and his brother John, Sir Walter Blunt and Falstaff. It is dawn on the day of battle. Henry observes how 'bloodily the sun begins to peer' over the hill, making the day seem pale. Hal adds that the whistling wind promises 'a tempest and a blust'ring day'. As so often in Shakespeare, disorder in the heavens accompanies disorder in human affairs.

Worcester and Vernon enter to give the rebels' answer to the King's peace terms. Henry greets him by saying that it is not well they should meet under such circumstances, Worcester having forced him to change the 'robes of peace' for the 'ungentle steel' of armour. He asks if Worcester is prepared to become an obedient subject once again. Worcester replies that he would be glad to live out his days in peace; he had not sought the rebellion. Falstaff's comment here ('Rebellion lay in his way, and he found it') punctures Worcester's claims of innocence.

Worcester tells a similar tale to Hotspur's in I V, iii. Henry, he says, has turned his favour from him and his family, even though they were his friends when he returned from exile. Henry swore that he had no designs on the throne, but this did not stop him usurping it when the circumstances were favourable. As a cuckoo takes advantage of a sparrow, so Henry took advantage of the Percys. Now they fear to be swallowed up by him; his hostility has forced them into rebellion.

We should not take the accounts of Worcester and Hotspur entirely at face value. The Percys' help to Henry could not have been entirely selfless; they hoped to increase their own power and prestige. Shakespeare twice recounts this tale of Henry's rise to the throne to remind us that he became king illegally and is tainted with the crime of which the Percys are now guilty. The present rebellion is in part a result of his own misdeeds in deposing an 'anointed king'.

Henry's reply, though, shows how the Percys have exploited their resentment of his power. He says that they have proclaimed throughout the kingdom their false reasons for rebellion, encouraging the poor and discontented to join them.

Hal steps forward to speak. Many men will die if the battle takes place, he says. He praises Hotspur for his bravery and chivalry, regretting his own lack of the same qualities. He issues a challenge: he will, in order to save the lives of many, face Hotspur 'in a single fight'.

Despite his love for his son, the King agrees to this. If the offer is accepted, he will pardon all the rebels. He dismisses Worcester and Vernon. Hal suspects the offer will be refused and the King therefore orders the final preparations for battle.

Falstaff and Hal are left on stage. Falstaff asks Hal to protect him if he sees him fallen in battle, but Hal replies with a curt joke and a dismissive farewell. Falstaff, in one of his most moving lines, wishes that it were time for bed and all were well. Hal's only comment is that Falstaff owes God a death; we see that he is too preoccupied with putting down the rebellion and resolving his rivalry with Hotspur to pay any attention to Falstaff now.

Alone, Falstaff delivers another monologue. Its subject is honour and its form a 'catechism' – question and answer. His attitude to honour is, of course, vastly different from that of Hotspur, or Vernon, or Hal. Unlike Hotspur's poetic ranting or Vernon's rich imagery, Falstaff's treatment of the theme consists of short questions and answers by means of which he 'proves' honour to be an utterly empty idea – 'a mere scutcheon' (a heraldic device, or funeral tablet). This view serves as a corrective to the extreme idea of honour that Hotspur holds, yet it is itself extreme – a licence for cowardice and treachery, for preserving one's own life at any cost. It is very funny, but we are not meant to see it as admirable. Falstaff's actions in the battle, based on his 'philosophy', show us that his idea of honour is as empty and dangerous as Hotspur's.

ACT V SCENE ii

In the rebel camp Worcester and Vernon are arguing about the King's proposal. Worcester says Hotspur must not know of this 'liberal and kind offer', while Vernon thinks he should be told. Worcester excuses his deceit by claiming that the King will not keep his word and pardon them. Hotspur's youth, he says, will excuse his actions, for which Northumberland and Worcester will be held responsible. Vernon agrees to withhold the information.

Hotspur enters with Douglas. Seeing his uncle, he orders Westmoreland, who is being held hostage, to be released and asks for news. Worcester says that the King will soon call them to battle, and Douglas goes to tell Westmoreland of the rebels' defiance. Worcester continues to lie, asserting that the King refuses to be merciful and claiming to have been diplomatic in his dealings with Henry – 'I told him gently of our grievances'.

Douglas returns. Worcester, as if ashamed of his dishonesty, now tells Hotspur that Hal has challenged him to single combat – but neglects to mention the King's offer of pardon. In lines of great irony Hotspur wishes that he and Hal might be the only two people to fight that day. He asks what kind of a figure Hal presented when making his challenge. Vernon's speech in reply is similar in mood to that of IV, i, in which he described Hal preparing for war. He recounts how

Hal made his challenge modestly, how he praised Hotspur graciously and sincerely, how critical he was of his own behaviour.

Hotspur can hardly believe it, given Hal's wild reputation. He calls his companions to arms, and reflects on the shortness of life. Yet, he continues, a life of even one hour would be too long if lived dishonourably. If they survive, they will master kings; if they die, it will have been an honourable death.

A messenger enters to warn of the King's approach. Hotspur thanks him and encourages his men to do their best. Drawing his sword, he shouts the Percys' battle-cry. The trumpets sound as they go to meet the King.

ACT V SCENE iii

The battle begins. Both this and the following scene are marked by rapid entrances and exits which convey something of the confusion of medieval warfare.

After the King and his soldiers have moved off, Sir Walter Blunt enters disguised as Henry, as are several others. Douglas follows his entrance, and Blunt asks who he is and what honour he seeks from him. Douglas says he seeks him because some say he is the King. Blunt affirms that he is, to which Douglas replies that he has already slain Stafford who was also disguised as Henry. He calls on Blunt to yield. As we would expect of him, he refuses. They fight and Blunt is killed.

Hotspur now makes his entry and praises Douglas's courage in battle. Douglas is jubilant because he believes he has killed the King and so won the battle. Hotspur, seeing Blunt's body, tells him that he has, in fact, killed Blunt and that the King 'hath many marching in his coats'. I'll murder them all, says Douglas, until I find the King himself.

In great contrast to the heroism and bravery we have just seen, Falstaff now makes his appearance. He notices Blunt's body and sees in his death proof of his own theory of honour. How 'honourable' Falstaff is we see from his next comments. He has 'led' his soldiers to their deaths, and only three out of a hundred and fifty remain. We must be careful not to misunderstand Falstaff's 'I have led . . .'; rather than fighting with his men, Falstaff has probably sent them to a part of the battlefield where he knew they would be killed so that he can now collect the pay of the dead men. His cynical dismissal of their fate is a further sharp reminder of his corruption.

Hal enters and asks why Falstaff is doing nothing when so many brave soldiers have died. He asks to borrow Falstaff's sword. Falstaff asks for time to recover from the heroic deeds he has performed, one of which is the killing of Hotspur. Hal ignores this outrageous lie and asks again for a sword. Falstaff offers instead a pistol, but in the holster Hal finds a bottle of wine. Asking if this is a time to joke, Hal throws the bottle at him and leaves. Falstaff, alone again, reaffirms his dislike of 'such grinning honour as Sir Walter hath'. He wishes to cling to life, no matter how dishonourably.

ACT V SCENE iv

The penultimate scene is the climax of the play, for in it Hal and Hotspur finally come face to face and resolve not only their personal rivalry but also the fate of the nation. Here, too, the debate about the nature of honour that has run through the play is resolved. Hotspur's obsessive and egotistical version does combat with the more balanced, and selfless, ideal embodied by Hal. In the background Falstaff, whose notion of honour is completely empty, provides a grotesque and ironic commentary on their struggle.

The scene opens with the King urging Hal to retire from the battle because of his wounds. Hal heroically refuses to do so. Prince John and Westmoreland leave, and Hal praises his younger brother's bravery, the King adding that he saw him valiantly fight off Hotspur. Hal returns to the battle.

Douglas enters, and asks who Henry is ('What art thou/That counterfeit'st the person of a king?'). Henry assures him that he is in fact the King, and they begin to fight. Hal enters to save his father, the King being in danger. He fights with Douglas, who escapes. The King tells Hal that he has redeemed himself and shown that he values his father's life. Hal replies that those who said he wished for his father's death did him a gross injustice. The King then leaves to support his forces in another part of the field.

At this point Hotspur enters. Hal says he is 'a very valiant rebel', but that they can no longer share in glory. Two stars cannot move in one course and England cannot have 'a double reign' of Hal and Hotspur. It shall not, replies Hotspur, 'for the hour is come/To end the one of us'. Hotspur wishes that Hal's reputation in arms were greater. Hal says that it will be before he leaves, for by defeating Hotspur he will win all his honour. Hotspur says he cannot bear such 'vanities' (boasts) and they engage in combat. Here Falstaff enters. He calls out flippant encouragement to Hal but is interrupted by the arrival of Douglas, who, without a word, begins to fight with him. Falstaff drops as if he were dead, thus saving his life but certainly not increasing our opinion of his bravery. Douglas rushes off and our attention returns to the combat between Hal and Hotspur.

Hal fatally wounds Hotspur. Even in his dying speech, Hotspur clings to his obsession with honour. He can better bear the loss of his life, he says, than the loss of the honour ('those proud titles') Hal has gained by defeating him. He dies with great dignity.

There is no gloating in Hal's speech over the dead body. He praises Hotspur's 'great heart' and contrasts his life and death. He covers Hotspur's face with his own 'favours' (a silk scarf worn around the helmet). From the corpse of his adversary Hal turns to Falstaff, whom he has just noticed and takes for dead. We should not be surprised, after his great struggle and the solemnity of his speech over Hotspur's body, that Hal is not more moved here. He would be more upset, he says, if he were 'much in love with vanity'; but his actions in battle have shown that he is not, and he does not at this time feel a great love for Falstaff.

Falstaff's 'resurrection' after Hal's exit is a great comic moment; watching the play for the first time, an audience would not know that he had only been feigning death. He explains that it was time for him to 'counterfeit' or Douglas would have killed him ('The better part of valour is discretion, in the which better part I have saved my life'). He then sees Hotspur's body and commits an act which almost completely removes any pleasure we may have felt at his 'resurrection'. In order to claim the honour and reward for Hotspur's death, he stabs him and lifts up the dead body.

Hal and Prince John enter, the former praising his younger brother for his bravery (thus throwing into relief Falstaff's shameful act). Both are amazed to see Falstaff alive. He throws the body down and says he expects to be rewarded by being made 'earl or duke'. When Hal says that he himself killed Hotspur, Falstaff replies instantly with out-rageous lies; again it is hard not to admire his audacity in concocting an unlikely tale. Although Hal is well aware that Falstaff's story is untrue, he is not angry with him and even offers to help him. We see that he has not yet tired completely of Falstaff's company.

They hear a trumpet sounding retreat, and they know then that they have won the battle. Hal and his brother go to see who of their companions is living and who has been killed.

Falstaff remains and tells us that if he is rewarded he will repent and 'live cleanly as a nobleman should do'. From what we have seen of Falstaff in the play, it is impossible to believe him.

ACT V SCENE v

The King and his supporters enter, with Worcester and Vernon prisoner. The King criticizes Worcester for his deceit in not telling Hotspur of his offer of clemency. If he had, says Henry, many men might not have died. Worcester admits that his actions were dictated by a desire for his own safety; throughout the play we have seen him acting out of narrow self-interest. Henry orders Vernon and Worcester to be executed. He asks for a report on the day. Hal replies that Douglas, seeing that the battle was lost and his soldiers were retreating in panic, fled and was later captured. The King allows Hal to 'dispose of him', which he does by ordering his brother John to give him his freedom, as a sign of Hal's high esteem for his bravery ('to you/This honourable bounty shall belong').

The play ends with the King dividing his army. Prince John and Westmoreland are to face Northumberland and the Archbishop of York, while Henry and Hal travel towards Wales to fight with Glendower and Mortimer. The play, then, does not end on a note of finality; the King has won a battle, but not the war. The final crushing of the rebellion, and Hal's abandonment of Falstaff, Shakespeare was to leave for *Henry IV, Part II*.

Characters

HAL

Hal is the central character in *1 Henry IV*, the focal point of the play's major themes. In his progress to maturity we see him resolve the opposing versions of honour represented by Hotspur and Falstaff. We see a prince's education as he learns the nature and responsibilities of kingship. Hal's relationship with Falstaff and his rivalry with Hotspur are essential to this education and the development of his character. At the beginning of the play, we see the King drawing a clear contrast between Hotspur and his son, whose reputation is sullied by 'riot and dishonour'; immediately after this opening scene we see Hal as, apparently, the bosom companion of Falstaff. He is thus balanced between these two extremes and we watch him to see which way he will turn. In Act I Scene ii, when we first see Hal, his relationship with Falstaff seems to be one of great intimacy. We are almost prepared to believe that this is the *real* Hal, yet, if we are alert, we notice in the jokes several hints that Hal is carefully maintaining his distance from Falstaff. His references to the gallows and the 'buff jerkin' worn by prisoners are reminders to Falstaff of what can happen to criminals. His outrage at Falstaff's suggestion that he has been more than friendly with the Hostess is a reminder to the audience that he is not completely dissolute. Hal, though, certainly enjoys Falstaff's company, his joking and high spirits. His initial distaste at the thought of taking part in the robbery is overcome by Poins's promise of the fun that will be provided by Falstaff's 'incomprehensible lies'.

If we do not catch the hints provided by Hal's sharp jokes, then his soliloquy at the end of I, ii provides a reassurance that he is not a rake, that he knows where his responsibilities ultimately lie. This is a knowledge, however, that he will only come to grasp fully in the course of the play. Indeed, it is a speech that betrays one of his faults – his immaturity. For just as Hotspur is over-anxious to monopolize honour, Hal here seems over-anxious to present his reformation in the most dramatic way.

We see more deeply into Hal's relationship with Falstaff in Act I I Scene iv. After enjoying Falstaff's fabrications and revealing the truth about what took place at Gad's Hill, Hal and Falstaff exchange the roles of king and prince in an extempore piece of play-acting. When Hal takes over the role of his father he gives a harsh opinion of Falstaff, who is shown as a devil leading the young Prince astray. While Hal is only acting, we should realize that he must at least partly share this view himself. When, still playing the King, he says he will banish Falstaff, we understand that this is what he will eventually have to do when he succeeds to the throne.

It is significant that this very serious play-acting occurs immediately after Hal has been told that the rebellion has broken out. This news makes him accept where his responsibilities lie; we now see him turning from the anarchic mock father-figure of Falstaff towards his real father, who represents values of order and responsibility which Hal has hitherto seemed to ignore.

The reconciliation scene with the King (I I I, ii) marks the turning-point in Hal's development. It is a decisive step away from Falstaff and towards his destiny. Hal listens patiently and submissively as his father recounts his faults and gives him a lesson in regal behaviour. When Hal says 'I shall hereafter . . ./Be more myself', it is a promise to assume the responsibilities and bearing that his birth as a prince demand. His father's praise of Hotspur leads to Hal's long speech in which he solemnly swears to redeem himself. Here the two themes of his rivalry with Hotspur and his own regeneration become more closely linked. Previously (I I, iv, 98) he had parodied Hotspur as a murderous lunatic; now we see that his real opinion holds him in much higher esteem and that he himself must win Hotspur's honours as a public sign of his change of heart. He will redeem himself 'on Percy's head' and the blood of battle will wash away his sins. Hal's wish that his own sins were even greater so that his defeat of Hotspur might appear even more glorious is further evidence of the immaturity we have already noticed in the soliloquy of I, ii. By linking Hal's reformation so closely to his rivalry with Hotspur, Shakespeare prepares us for the climax of the play – their single combat in Act V.

Having made his peace with his father Hal is now seen to be resolute in his determination to crush the rebellion (and Hotspur). There is a new sense of urgency and seriousness in his appearances throughout the second half of the play. As he assumes his responsibilities he becomes more aware of Falstaff's shortcomings and his criticisms of him become sharper. In I I I, iii he is less appreciative of the humour of Falstaff's insolence and lying than he was earlier in the play. He has a much clearer view of Falstaff's corruption: '. . . there's no room for faith, truth, nor honesty in this bosom of thine', he says, and adds, 'Art thou not ashamed?' (I I I, iii, 156).

Hal's new role as soldier is emphasized in I V, i by Vernon's description of his preparations. Hal is presented as the very essence of chivalry – 'plumed', 'glittering', vaulting on to his horse with matchless ease. Hotspur's pained reaction increases our understanding of the rivalry between the two young men. In I, iii he had described Hal as the 'sword-and-buckler Prince of Wales'; that is, a nobleman debasing himself by using the weapons of the serving man. Now he hears the 'madcap' described as a worthy competitor for the honour he wishes to monopolize. It is clear that they must resolve their rivalry in battle.

The newly chivalrous Hal is again shown in V, i when he makes his offer of single combat with Hotspur. He wishes not only to resolve their personal struggle, but also to save unnecessary bloodshed; it is not merely a selfish challenge. Hal shows his high opinion of Hotspur, completely different from the parody of I I, iv. Later in this scene we notice once more his growing estrangement from Falstaff. His last words to him before the battle are a curt 'thou owest God a death'. At this crucial moment Hal has no time for Falstaff.

Vernon again praises Hal (V, ii), making much of the modesty and elegance of his challenge. We cannot avoid comparing Hal with the intemperate Hotspur, and we notice how much Hal has changed. Even the rebel Vernon is moved to say, 'If he outlive the envy of this day,/England did never owe so sweet a hope,/So much misconstrued in his wantonness', acknowledging that Hal has the makings of a good king.

In battle Hal distinguishes himself and, indeed, marks his repentance with blood. When, in the midst of battle, Falstaff meets Hal and offers him a bottle of wine instead of a weapon, Hal angrily throws it back, underlining the desperate circumstances by his question, '. . . is it a time to jest and dally now?' Hal has realized when play must stop and serious life begin, but Falstaff has not.

Hal's heroism is further stressed when the King begs him to rest. Despite his wounds Hal refuses to do so while the battle remains to be won. When he saves the King's life by defeating Douglas the reconciliation between father and son is complete; until this moment Henry has had some doubts about the sincerity of Hal's repentance.

Now Hotspur enters and the play reaches its climax. We see the full extent of the rivalry as Hal says that England cannot brook 'a double reign/Of Harry Percy and the Prince of Wales'. Hal's speech over the defeated Hotspur's body is full of generosity. He does not gloat over the honour he has won, but rather shows a mature understanding of Hotspur's greatness and limitations. Hal turns away from his great adversary only to find Falstaff, apparently dead. His farewell to him is touching, yet balanced. After the death of so many more worthy men, Hal does not over-react. He shows his awareness of Falstaff's shortcomings, saying he would miss him more if he were 'much in love with vanity'. When, a few moments later, he finds Falstaff alive, he is happy but not overjoyed. Hal has not yet completely tired of Falstaff and he is prepared to go along with the lie that Falstaff has killed Hotspur. Hal's final act in the play is to give Douglas his freedom, as a mark of esteem for his courage.

The Hal we see at the beginning of the play is a young man who is still learning what it means to be adult, to have responsibilities. This universal problem is for him unusually difficult to resolve; Hal is not just any young man, but a prince. As such, the adult responsibility he will have to bear is the heavy one of governing a nation. He must learn how to rule and how to maintain order in the face of the constant threat of anarchy. Hotspur and Falstaff, while having different versions of honour, both represent rebellion. Between them we see Hal steering a course which preserves order without abandoning honour. Hal shows us that both Hotspur's and Falstaff's ideas of honour are inadequate; the former are disruptive in their single-minded obsession, the latter in their cynical self-interest. Hal learns from both, but in the end he embodies a different kind of honour, one that is aware of the human cost of war without being dismissive of the necessity for integrity and bravery.

His experience in the world of the tavern has helped him to learn this lesson. Here Hal develops a sympathy and humanity which his father lacks. We see it in I I, iv where he becomes 'sworn brother to a leash of drawers' who regard him as 'no proud Jack like Falstaff, but a Corinthian, a lad of mettle'. Although his attitude to them is ironic, he has undergone a broadening of his experience and sympathies. His father does not understand this; Henry sees only indulgence in vulgar pleasures in Hal's frequenting the tavern (I I, ii). We notice, however, the ease with which Hal moves between the different worlds of court, tavern and battle. This understanding of various aspects of the kingdom is what will make Hal a good monarch.

Hal learns from his father the necessity of maintaining order in the kingdom and of preserving the dignity of the king. For these reasons he must move away from Falstaff. We do not think Hal heartless as he speaks over Falstaff's 'dead' body because we realize his duty is incompatible with a great love for the corrupt and anarchic Falstaff.

In the course of *1 Henry IV* we see Hal progress from an immature and carefree state to an adult acceptance of his responsibilities. The rebellion of the Percys provides the occasion for him to develop, as it highlights the danger of disorder and allows Hal to see the threat to society posed by the extremes of Hotspur and Falstaff. Hal's tavern companions have played an essential part in his education, but he must eventually discard them. At the end of the play he has not completely broken with Falstaff, as we see from his promise to 'gild' Falstaff's lie that he has killed Hotspur. But we know that he has grown up and that he will prove to be a better, more human king than his father.

HOTSPUR

As his nickname Hotspur suggests, Harry Percy is an impulsive and reckless character who acts first and thinks later. His bravery and rashness are the two qualities constantly commented on by the other characters in the play. Yet on the whole it is his bravery which impresses them most; for them, he is the epitome of honour, the living example of those chivalric values to which a noble youth should aspire. By the end of the play, however, we have had an opportunity to see Hotspur in perspective and our judgement of him is not so favourable. We realize that, brave and likeable as he is, his pursuit of honour is dangerously obsessive – so much so that it leads him to threaten the peace and unity of the kingdom.

The admirable side of Hotspur's nature is demonstrated in the very first scene of the play, before he himself has made an appearance. Westmoreland calls his victory over Douglas at Holmedon 'a conquest for a prince to boast of', prompting the King to a glowing description of Hotspur as 'the theme of honour's tongue'. The contrast between Hotspur and Hal which the King makes here is a major element in the play, and one of Hotspur's most important dramatic functions is to act, like Falstaff, as an extreme from whom Hal must take some qualities while rejecting others.

The King enlarges on his view of Hotspur later in the play (III, ii) and again it is to Hal's disadvantage. He compares Hal with Richard II and says 'as I was then is Percy now'. He credits Hotspur with a more 'worthy interest' (right by worth) to the throne than Hal, for he has proved himself many times in battle. Henry sees Percy as a young god of war – 'Mars in swathling clothes' – and says he is acknowledged by all as the holder of 'military title capital'. He is regarded as the greatest soldier in Europe.

To this high promise is added the testimony of many other characters. Glendower (in III, i) flatters Hotspur before he gets down to the serious business of flattering himself. Later in the same scene Mortimer reveals that only Hotspur's great reputation has restrained Glendower's anger. Another warrior of renown, Douglas, addresses

Hotspur as the 'king of honour' (IV, i). Such tributes from friend and enemy alike are more than enough to convince us that Hotspur's reputation for courage and honour is deserved.

There is, however, another side to this reputation, and it would be a mistake to invest Hotspur with a wholly admirable character. The impetuosity that is so valuable in battle leads him in more peaceful times to display a lack of judgement and maturity. These faults are also prompted by the pursuit of honour; he is obsessed with the idea to such an extent that he has no time to consider the consequences of his actions. Despite his integrity, his attitude to honour is selfishly irresponsible.

This unfavourable side of Hotspur is one that Henry has little opportunity to see. He knows only the Hotspur of famous deeds. An audience, however, is given the complete view, and can see Hotspur at home, at court and in battle. To this variety of circumstances can be added the way in which Shakespeare links the different worlds and characters of the play. Thus Falstaff's theory of honour comments on Hotspur's and helps us to form our opinion of it. Hotspur's rhetoric when describing the fight between Mortimer and Glendower (I, iii) should not be forgotten when Falstaff tells his 'incomprehensible lies' in II, iv; the latter helps us to put Hotspur's rant in perspective.

Hotspur's rashness and his obsession with honour are both clearly shown in his first appearance. The King's refusal to ransom Mortimer enrages him and his father has difficulty in preventing him from chasing after the King (I, iii, 125). He seems more angry about the offence to the Percys' pride than about any genuine wrongs Henry has committed (1, iii, 158–86) – the first suggestion that 'honour' urges him on to rebellion. He constantly interrupts his cooler uncle throughout the scene, unable to repress his feelings. As his father remarks: 'Imagination of some great exploit/Drives him beyond the bounds of patience.' Hotspur's attitude to honour is clearly outlined (1, iii, 201–8); he wishes to monopolize it, to have it all to himself. His outburst, 'But out upon this half-faced fellowship!', shows how immature, even childish, he is. When Worcester reveals the plot, Hotspur shows the kind of excitement a child might feel on being told of a trip to the zoo. This thrill at the thought of battle and honour precludes any serious consideration of what he is about to do, of what rebellion means for the nation. In the last lines of this scene he can think only of the 'sport' the rebellion will bring him.

This is the Hotspur we see quarrelling with Glendower (III, i): unable to bear listening to praise of Hal which might detract from his own supremacy in chivalry (IV, iii); over-eager to begin battle with superior forces. It is the side of Hotspur which Hal makes fun of when describing him as 'he that kills me some six or seven dozen of Scots at a breakfast' (II, iv, 98). This parody of Hotspur as a murderous, bloodthirsty maniac is not, of course, the whole truth; nor is it, as we see later in the play, Hal's considered judgement. It does, however, drive home the point that there is something very wrong with Hotspur's pursuit of honour; it is obsessive and dangerous.

The combative and rash side of Hotspur is balanced, to some extent, by those scenes in which he shows his tenderness towards his wife. In II, iii we see him at home. Kate's long speech (II, iii, 35–61) about his 'thick-eyed musing and cursed melancholy' reveals that Hotspur has at least some worries about the consequences of his actions, but his immaturity prevents him from coming to terms with them. Characteristically he ignores his wife and gives orders for his departure. The scene shows, too, the bond of affection between husband and wife. He does not openly state his feelings; they are expressed in flippant jokes, as if he wished to repress the more sensitive side of his nature (as also in III, i where he bids Kate farewell before going to Shrewsbury).

Hotspur's humour is, typically, robust and immature. When he thinks he has scored a point over Glendower, he gleefully repeats it several times as if it were a memorable witticism (III, i, 58). Funnier, if still not very sophisticated, is his parody (I, iii) of the officer 'perfumèd like a milliner' who demanded his prisoners at Holmedon. His enthusiastic portrayal of the fop momentarily wins him the sympathy of the audience (and of Sir Walter Blunt). But these more sympathetic aspects of Hotspur cannot completely redeem him. His uncle Worcester twice makes telling criticisms of him. In III, i he says Hotspur is too 'wilful-blame' which leads him to show 'pride, haughtiness, opinion and disdain' (III, i, 175–87). In V, ii he describes him as a 'hare-brained Hotspur, governed by a spleen' (impulse). It is this Hotspur who rebels against the King, not because of any great injustice but rather from a feeling that the family pride has been damaged (IV, iii) and from a desire to win yet more honours in battle. Although he wishes that the battle might be limited to himself and Hal (V, ii), it is more from a desire that the culmination of their rivalry should bring him more honour than from any mature wish to save lives.

Towards the end of the play, when his father and Glendower fail to arrive, his isolation becomes genuinely heroic. His death, too, is moving in its nobility. Yet even here we cannot help but notice the unbalanced and immature attitude that prompts him to say: 'I better brook the loss of brittle life/Than those proud titles thou hast won of me.'

FALSTAFF

Falstaff is one of the great comic characters in the world's dramatic literature. Since he first appeared, in *1 Henry IV*, audiences have loved him, laughed at him and clamoured for more of him. He is a larger-than-life character who seems to represent qualities of human nature we all share.

When we see a performance of *1 Henry IV* we are likely to be overwhelmed by the liveliness of Falstaff, by the way in which he and his view of the world seem to dominate the stage. This great energy in his personality can lead us to suspend our judgement. Falstaff is so *alive* that normal considerations of right or wrong do not seem to apply. We just accept him for what he is. When we study the play, however, we are able to reflect, discuss and make a more balanced assessment of him. We come to see that beneath his boisterous good humour he is a braggart, a glutton and a coward whose lies and jokes turn the virtues of the world upside down. We feel great affection for him, but we have to realize that the chaos he brings with him is dangerous as well as comic.

Falstaff and his companions form a low-life world which acts as a powerful contrast to, and comment on, the play's other worlds of honour, power and kingship. While the King and the rebels concern themselves with serious questions of justice, chivalry and the possession of the kingdom, Falstaff and his friends are preoccupied with drink, jests and money. Throughout the play Falstaff's appearances are juxtaposed with scenes of seriousness and importance, always with sharp dramatic effect.

We first meet Falstaff in the tavern, immediately after the solemn opening scene of the play. The tavern, in fact, seems to be Falstaff's natural habitat. He is completely at home there. When we see him later, at the Battle of Shrewsbury, he is ill at ease in the unfamiliar surroundings and serious atmosphere.

In Act I Scene ii Shakespeare quickly establishes the nature of Falstaff's relationship with Hal. At first we are surprised to see the heir to the throne in such a close relationship with a man who is clearly a disreputable buffoon, but with great skill Shakespeare shows how, in spite of their intimacy, Hal maintains his distance. Falstaff, waking up, asks for the time, and Hal mocks him by saying that time as measured by the clock has nothing to do with Falstaff. For him, time should be measured by drink, food and women (I, ii, 6).

We are thus immediately given a clear picture of Falstaff's interests in life. At this point Falstaff seems to be very close to Hal; he calls him 'sweet wag' and 'lad', terms of great familiarity to use to the heir to the throne. He jokes with Hal and can even make fun of him, but, like a court jester, he can only go so far. When he oversteps the mark Hal quickly reasserts his dignity and makes clear the gulf in social status that separates them. In this way Hal prepares us for his speech at the end of the scene, in which he foreshadows a break with Falstaff and his companions. His complicated joke about 'a buff jerkin' (1, ii, 40) is a way of telling Falstaff; 'Watch you don't end up in jail', and also of reminding him of the distance between them.

This scene also shows Falstaff's great affection for Hal. It is clear that Falstaff needs Hal, whereas Hal can do without Falstaff. We get the impression that Falstaff regards the Prince as the son he never had.

Falstaff has a comical habit of blaming others for the troubles he has brought on himself. He even accuses Hal of having corrupted him (I, ii, 85). The irony, of course, is that Falstaff is really the corrupter Hal must resist in order to develop the qualities of kingship. Falstaff undertakes to give up his sinful life, only to fall into a trap prepared by Hal who invites him to join in a robbery (I, ii, 93). Falstaff forgets repentance and eagerly, almost childishly, agrees to take part. Poins enters, and we learn of the practical joke that is to be played on Falstaff, for the sake of the 'incomprehensible lies' he will afterwards tell.

Until Falstaff's next appearance, in Act II Scene ii, we have been amused mainly by his conversation. Although we cannot fail to notice his huge physical presence, he has not really *used* it for any comic or dramatic purpose. Now, at Gad's Hill, we see him in a different element, away from the tavern, and he seems to flounder like a fish out of water. His first appearance in this scene is funny primarily because of his size. Poins has hidden his horse and Falstaff is thrown into despair by the problems this will cause him. When Hal enters and tells Falstaff to lie down and listen for the victims' footsteps, Falstaff displays one of his most endearing qualities – the ability to laugh at himself. He asks, 'Have you any levers to lift me up again, being down?' (II, ii, 32). At the travellers' entry we see another side of Falstaff: the blustering would-be highwayman. He hides his own fear by yelling bloodthirsty encouragement to his companions (II, ii, 77). We are unlikely to take Falstaff very seriously here. Although he would like to have a fearsome reputation, his words always speak much louder than his actions. He regards the robbery – indeed his whole life – as a game to be enjoyed as much as possible. In the early scenes of the play this attitude makes us laugh. In the later scenes, Shakespeare shows us how dangerous and irresponsible it can be. When Hal and Poins enter to rob the robbers, Falstaff's bravery disappears. He runs away, no doubt shrieking and wailing ridiculously, thus preparing us for his dishonourable behaviour in the battle scenes later in the play.

The point of the Gad's Hill joke comes in Act II Scene iv, a great comic scene which we can divide into two parts. First comes Falstaff's story, and, second, the play-acting in which Falstaff and Hal exchange the roles of King and Prince.

The first half of the scene bears out all Poins's predictions about Falstaff's 'incomprehensible lies'. Falstaff enters, ignoring Hal and Poins and complaining of the cowardice of the world. He even considers himself to be one of the few virtuous men alive (II, iv, 122). Prompted by Hal, Falstaff explains his hurt feelings. His lies become more and more absurd. As we learn later, Falstaff has carefully prepared his story; he has broken his sword and persuaded his companions to bloody their own noses and clothes. Yet as he tells these outrageous lies he cannot help being carried away by his own delight in 'spinning a yarn'. A dozen becomes 'sixteen at least'. Two men in buckram quickly become four, then seven. Falstaff is unworried by his contradictions being noticed – he just brushes objections aside and steams ahead.

We enjoy this performance all the more for knowing, with Hal and Poins, that the story is a pack of lies. This shared knowledge makes it all the funnier when Hal finally halts Falstaff by revealing that he knows the truth. We can imagine a long, suspense-filled pause after Poins has asked Falstaff, 'What trick hast thou now?' (II, iv, 252). Typically quick-witted and shameless, Falstaff replies that he knew very well who the robbers were, and produces a list of incredible reasons why he *had* to run away. We are unlikely, at this point, to consider whether Falstaff has behaved in a cowardly way or not; we are more concerned to enjoy seeing him embellish his story to appear more heroic. The irony of Falstaff pretending to be a hero is important, as one of his major dramatic functions is to act as a balance to the idea of honour held by such characters as Hotspur and Blunt.

When Falstaff and Hal take turns at playing King and Prince in the second half of Act II Scene iv we gain another insight into their relationship. Coming after the news that the rebellion has begun in earnest, it is both comic and touching. Playing the King, Falstaff describes himself as a man of great virtue (line 405). It is a sign of Falstaff's lack of self-knowledge that he seems to believe this.

This view is corrected, though, when Hal reverses the roles; Falstaff will be the Prince, and Hal the King. We now see Falstaff as he must appear to Henry IV: a gross, fat old man who is corrupting the heir to the throne (line 439). This must also reflect, to a certain extent, Hal's own opinion of Falstaff. The audience, too, is influenced and we begin to view Falstaff more critically. Falstaff is obviously hurt but, irrepressible as ever, he is eloquent in his defence (line 450). The last lines of the 'play' (line 456) contain great pathos. We know that Hal will, must, break with Falstaff; he is aware that his responsibilities as heir-apparent will not allow him to be too closely identified with Falstaff. Falstaff, though, has no such insight. For him, life will continue to be one long game. As the situation in the country becomes more critical, we begin to see how irresponsible this attitude is.

At the end of Scene iv, after the Sheriff has entered and departed, Falstaff is discovered asleep, 'snorting like a horse'. Hal reads out a bill which reveals Falstaff's enormous appetites: gallons of wine and 'one halfpennyworth of bread'. References to Falstaff's size continue in Act III Scene iii. Here he seems to be in a subdued mood. He asks Bardolph if he thinks he has lost weight; the idea is ridiculous, but Falstaff enlarges on it, comparing himself with things either tiny or notoriously thin. He even claims to have been as thin as Hal in his youth, although an audience would probably find it hard to believe Falstaff had *ever* been slim.

We should notice here that the scene immediately preceding this is the crucial one in which Hal begs his father's forgiveness; he has realized the gravity of the situation. From this solemn moment we are transported to the tavern where Falstaff, as ever, is joking with his friends. The contrast is clear. It is important to see that while Falstaff acts as a comic balance to the other parts and ideas in the play, they in their turn help us to see him more critically. From this turning-point in the action of the play Falstaff is presented much more savagely. As the rebellion gathers force we are less likely to see him simply as a figure of fun but more as a threat to the success of the King's enterprise.

Hal has got Falstaff his 'charge of foot' (infantry) and Falstaff's behaviour as captain shows some of the more serious defects of his character as well as of the military system. In Act IV Scene ii we find

Falstaff and Bardolph on the march to Shrewsbury with their soldiers and discover how Falstaff has recruited them. They are so 'dishonour-able-ragged' that even Falstaff is ashamed of them (IV, ii, 11). Falstaff is here damned out of his own mouth. In order to line his own pocket he has allowed more able-bodied men to buy their way out and has re-placed them with the poorest and weakest – those most unfit to fight well. His irresponsibility is not just harmless fun; the country is torn by civil war and it is Falstaff's duty to supply the best soldiers he can, which he obviously has not done. Despite its very serious purpose, this monologue of Falstaff's is still very funny, above all because of the vividness with which he describes his soldiers. His attitude towards them is shown later in the scene when Hal and Westmoreland criticize them. Falstaff shamelessly replies that they are just cannon-fodder (line 63). They will be used up so that he himself can collect their pay (Act V Scene iii).

From recruiting, Falstaff moves on to the actual scene of battle and it would be hard to imagine a more unlikely soldier. Here we see his importance as a critic of the idea of honour. Hotspur's single-minded kind of honour is blind and dangerous, and Falstaff gives a witty criticism of it at the end of Act V Scene i. His speech is in question-and-answer form, a 'catechism'; by the end of it he has 'proved' honour to be an empty idea, 'a mere scutcheon' (line 139). This does not mean that Shakespeare regards honour as nonsense; Hotspur's version of honour is balanced by Falstaff's equally extreme view.

With this notion of honour – which really means saving his own skin – Falstaff takes part in the battle. We learn that most of his soldiers are dead (V, iii, 36). The suggestion is not that Falstaff led them in battle, but that he took them to a place where he knew they would be slaughtered and then took cover. This flippant dismissal shows again that, despite the desperate circumstances, Falstaff is unable to act in a serious and adult manner. As Hal says when Falstaff offers him a bottle of wine instead of the pistol he should be carrying, 'What, is it a time to jest and dally now?' (V, iii, 54). Of course it is not, but Falstaff is utterly incapable of seeing this.

As the play reaches its dramatic climax (the fight between Hal and

Hotspur), examples of genuine courage lead us to view Falstaff in a much harsher light. Even though his appearances are still amusing, we do not view him as lightly as we did earlier in the play. Circumstances have changed, but Falstaff has not.

In Act V Scene iv Falstaff is challenged by Douglas and 'falls down as if he were dead'. His 'corpse' provides a silent and ironic commentary on Hotspur's last words. We see in Hal's speech over Falstaff how weak the bond between them is; although there is a certain tenderness in Hal's words, he sheds no unnecessary tears and is sufficiently unmoved to make a pun (line 104) on the word 'heavy'.

Falstaff's later 'resurrection' is a moment of great comedy, especially as an audience might not know he was only feigning death. In his monologue (V, iv, 110) he wittily expounds his theory of 'honour' once again. Our laughter, though, is cut short. The developing criticism of Falstaff turns to disgust when he commits the repellent act of stabbing Hotspur and claiming the honour of killing him. We now see that Falstaff can be vicious and cruel, that his ideas of honour are as dangerous and irresponsible as Hotspur's. By his deceit Falstaff hopes to be rewarded by being made 'either earl or duke'.

In his final words in the play (V, iv, 159), he vows to reform. It is unlikely that many people believe him. We feel that Falstaff will not, cannot, change. Unlike most important characters in Shakespeare's plays (Hal, for instance) Falstaff shows no development; he is the same at the end of the play as he was at the beginning. Despite civil war and many deaths, Falstaff has learned nothing from his experiences.

What has changed, though, is our view of him. When, near the beginning of the play, we see Falstaff in the tavern and at Gad's Hill we are won over by the great comedy that springs from his irresponsibility. But as the rebellion progresses Falstaff's attitude remains the same. He is still funny, but our laughter is more thoughtful. We realize that his response to the dire state of the nation is completely inadequate. His cynical attitude to the recruits and his cowardly behaviour at Shrewsbury reinforce our harsher view.

From Falstaff's almost childish irresponsibility come both his good and bad points. We enjoy his humour and his high spirits, his energy and love of life. But the other side of this coin is his lack of awareness of any more important issues than his own pleasure and safety. He cannot see that, in order to be a good ruler, Hal will have to break with him. He cannot see how his own behaviour in the war is selfish and damaging to the nation. Shakespeare very skilfully emphasizes these bad aspects of Falstaff's character so that we should not be too swayed by the affection we feel for him.

By the end of the play we realize that Falstaff is not the harmless joker we might have thought him earlier. Beneath his jovial blustering he can be heartless, selfish and dangerous. Despite this disapproval we still want to see more of him, perhaps because there is something of Falstaff in all of us. We probably would agree with his words to Hal: 'Banish plump Jack, and banish all the world' (I I, iv, 455).

HENRY IV

At the beginning of the play Henry appears to be a tired and weak man. Like his kingdom, he is 'shaken' and 'wan with care'. We learn later that he became king by deposing Richard I I, who had subsequently been murdered (though not on Henry's orders). To heal the wounds of the country he has proposed a crusade to the Holy Land. Another reason for this, although it is not given in his opening speech, is the guilt he feels for his illegal accession to the throne and for Richard's murder. Remorse, however, is not Henry's only trouble; after Welsh and Scottish wars his own great noblemen are proving to be unruly. Moreover, his son and heir has acquired a reputation for debauchery and seems unlikely to make a good king. Such problems are made more acute by Henry's old age.

Little of Henry's private self is revealed in the play. His main role is as a figure of authority, both regal and paternal. For the most part he appears as a reserved, rather cold figure, lacking the warmth or spontaneity of Hotspur or Hal.

The threat of rebellion at the beginning of the play rekindles Henry's sense of his responsibilities; a king must govern with strength or his noblemen will become over-ambitious. This is especially true when, as is the case with Henry, the king has won the crown through his own power rather than inheritance. At the beginning of Act I Scene iii we see a much more resolute and authoritative figure. Henry says he has been 'too cold and temperate'. Now, though, he will be more like a king, 'mighty, and to be feared ...' This he quickly proves by expelling Worcester from court. His determination to govern and stamp out rebellion continues throughout the play.

In the same scene we are given the first of four accounts of Henry's rise to the throne – three times the story is told by the rebels, and once by Henry himself.

Ignoring for the moment the different emphasis that each side gives to the story, we are told that, at the outset, Henry had returned from exile to claim his inheritance. Aided by the Percys, Richard's absence in Ireland and the disaffection of the population, he had become king. According to the rebels, their only motive in giving their support had been that Henry should have justice and receive his lands and titles. Both Hotspur (IV, iii, 52–105) and Worcester (V, i, 30–71) assert that the Percys helped only on the solemn understanding that Henry's ambition would not reach as high as to claim the crown. These assertions should be considered sceptically. As we have seen (I, iii), Hotspur knows only what his father and Worcester have told him. Worcester himself is portrayed as deceitful and self-interested. Hotspur also maintains (IV, iii) that, after deposing Richard, Henry 'deprived him of his life'. This, too, is rather extreme, as Henry was not directly responsible for Richard's death.

There is, though, some substance in the rebels' claims. When Henry himself tells the story of his rise (to Hal, in III, ii) he is careful not to include any details which might reflect badly on himself. He suggests that it was the contrast between Richard's corruption and his own regal bearing which brought him the throne.

What we may deduce from these two versions of the same story is that Henry has become king illegally. If he is not directly responsible for Richard's death, he at least bears the moral responsibility. Shakespeare returns to this tale several times so that we should not forget Henry's past misdeeds; we come to see that rebellion breeds rebellion.

The fact that Henry is suffering from remorse confirms the illegality of his rise. He reveals these feelings of guilt in the scene in which we most clearly see his humanity: the reconciliation with Hal (III, ii). Here he wonders if his son's misbehaviour is not 'the hot vengeance and the rod of heaven/To punish my mistreadings'. What these 'mistreadings' are he does not say, but he is clearly thinking of the overthrow and death of Richard II.

Henry's sadness and disappointment at Hal's behaviour move him to tears ('foolish tenderness'). But he is not just a father in this scene: his long speeches to Hal are as much a lesson in kingship as a father's reproof to a wayward son. The reconciliation of parent and child is indissoluble from the reconciliation of King and Prince. The King places his trust in Hal, giving him an important command in the army. We see something of their affection when, in Act V Scene iv, the King begs his son to rest and have treatment for his wounds. Yet the reconciliation is not complete until Hal defeats Douglas, thus showing that he genuinely values his father's life. Henry's words reveal that he had still harboured doubts about Hal's devotion (lines 46–9).

In Act I Scene iii Hotspur describes Henry as 'a vile politician' and 'a fawning greyhound'. Henry is certainly a politician, careful to present a good public image and concerned to maximize and maintain his power; we cannot accept his suggestion that he came to power by accident. Even the plan to go to the Holy Land may have an ulterior motive – foreign wars are a time-honoured method of diverting attention from domestic problems. Yet we do not believe Hotspur's extreme judgement or the rebels' claim that they are in revolt for fear that Henry will destroy them. For although Henry displays cool judgement throughout the play, we feel sympathy for him as he worries over the future of his country and of his son; Hal's development and the country's well-being are inseparably linked. When in Act V Scene i Hal offers single combat with Hotspur as a way of avoiding widespread bloodshed, we believe Henry's offer of mercy. Even Worcester calls it a 'kind and liberal offer'.

Although we cannot forget Henry's guilty acquisition of power, we have to respect the way in which he uses it. As a king, he does what he has to do. It is from his son that we expect a warmer, more human style of leadership.

WORCESTER

In contrast to most of the other important characters in the play, it is not difficult to make a firm judgement on Worcester. Unlike Falstaff or Hotspur, there is no ambiguity in the way he is presented. From the very beginning we see him as a cold and malicious schemer, concerned only for his own advantage. His character develops only to the extent that our opinion of him is even lower at the end of the play than it was at the beginning.

In Act I Scene i we learn from Blunt that Westmoreland is bitterly opposed to Henry (line 96), and this opinion is confirmed by Worcester's behaviour in Scene iii. He insolently reminds Henry how the Percys helped him to the throne. After his expulsion he returns to Hotspur and Northumberland and we see that he is the prime mover behind the rebellion. The plot is so far advanced that it must have been in preparation for some time; the present argument over Hotspur's prisoners and Mortimer's ransom is only a pretext for Worcester. He coolly lays out the details of the plot, showing impatience only at Hotspur's repeated outbursts. His reasons for rebellion – that the Percys must remove Henry before he removes them – lack any evidence to support them.

We do not see Worcester again until the second half of the play. His only contribution to the scene in which the rebels divide the kingdom (I I I, i) is an acute assessment of Hotspur's character. Worcester is, of course, temperamentally the opposite of Hotspur: thoughtful, devious and deceitful. His prudence is emphasized in the rebels' discussions at Shrewsbury. When Northumberland and Glendower fail to arrive, he is much more aware than Hotspur of the blow to their enterprise in both military and political terms (IV, i). In Act IV Scene iii we see him almost lose his temper as he argues with Hotspur on when to give battle; Worcester, of course, favours waiting for reinforcements. In Act V Scene i his claim not to have sought the 'day of this dislike' is punctured by Falstaff's sharp joke, with the result that it is impossible for us to believe his pious speech about Henry's injustices. The King makes the 'liberal and kind offer' of mercy if Hotspur will accept Hal's challenge. Now we see Worcester in the worst possible light as he refuses to tell Hotspur of the offer (V, ii). For his own safety he is prepared to see many men die. His low opinion of Hotspur is evident; there is an air of contempt in his description of him as a 'hare-brained Hotspur, governed by a spleen'.

His deceit is rewarded, however, by capture and death. Henry rebukes him for his lies and Worcester replies, 'What I have done my safety urged me to'. His only fine moment in the play is the calm with which he accepts the news of his death sentence.

Worcester, then, cannot be seen as anything other than a villain. His rebellion is prompted by envy and self-interest. He is deceitful and manipulative, using Hotspur's sense of honour for his own base ends. What Worcester thinks of honour can be seen by his refusal to tell Hotspur of the King's offer. Hotspur calls Henry 'a vile politician' (I, iii); but it is a description much more suitable for his uncle, Worcester.

NORTHUMBERLAND

Northumberland appears in only one scene (I, iii), and even here he does not say much. We have the impression that, like the King, he is an old man, now reliving his youth through his son.

He is reticent, as is Worcester, about the major part he played in bringing about Richard II's downfall. His involvement is now masked by an air of pious repentance we know to be hypocritical (I, iii, 147–52). He is content to let Worcester take the leading role in the conspiracy, assenting by his silence to the unconvincing reasons given – that they must depose Henry before he destroys them. As we might expect of a father, he is aware of his son's more glaring faults. Several times in this scene he gives acute criticisms of Hotspur (lines 129, 199, 235 and 272). Despite his involvement in two rebellions, Northumberland seems to have no awareness of the cost to the country of his actions.

After this scene we hear of him again in Act I V Scene i, when Hotspur receives the letter telling of his sickness. It is interesting that Northumberland does not send his troops under another's command. Worcester fears it will be thought 'That wisdom, loyalty, and mere dislike/Of our proceedings kept the earl from hence'; we may well suspect there is some selfish motive in Northumberland's absence.

GLENDOWER

Although, like Northumberland, Glendower appears in only one scene he is a forceful and vivid character. He brings to the play the exotic air of a land where Merlin and fabulous beasts are realities, where noblemen learn poetry and magic as well as the arts of war.

His reputation is mentioned in Act I Scene iii; Hotspur calls him 'great Glendower' when describing the heroic struggle Mortimer had with him. Henry refuses to believe the story since 'he durst as well have met the devil alone/As Owen Glendower for an enemy'. His reputation is not only for valour but also for supernatural powers. When we eventually see him (I I I, i), we learn that Glendower is also boastful and arrogant. In language full of imagery he tells Hotspur he is 'not in the roll of common men'. Comically, Hotspur's taunts only provoke him to even wilder boasts. But we see his more chivalrous side as he translates his daughter's Welsh for Mortimer and conjures up music of such beauty that even Hotspur is compelled to praise it. Hotspur's complaint of Glendower's tedious boasting (I I I, i, 146–62) is balanced by Mortimer's praise of his virtues (I I I, i, 163–74).

It is a measure of Shakespeare's dramatic and poetic genius that, despite the brevity of his appearance, Glendower is a memorable and clearly defined character.

BARDOLPH, PETO, POINS, MISTRESS QUICKLY, FRANCIS, THE TWO CARRIERS

Of Falstaff's companions Bardolph is the most clearly defined. This is due chiefly to his most noticeable physical characteristic – his glowing red face. This is a feature Falstaff makes much of in Act III Scene iii when Bardolph has displeased him. Bardolph's face is like 'the lantern in the poop' he says, adding, 'I never see thy face but I think upon hellfire . . .' Apart from this distinguishing feature, Bardolph is not drawn in any great depth. He does Falstaff's bidding (as in Act IV Scene ii when Falstaff sends him, without money, to get more wine) and occasionally makes a rebelliously insolent remark. Peto is a sketchier character than Bardolph. He is a hanger-on who goes along with whatever is suggested.

Poins is rather different. He seems to have a position as personal servant to Hal, and is thus set apart from the inhabitants of the tavern. Like Hal he sees Falstaff in a more critical light than Bardolph and Peto. In Act I Scene ii it is he who organizes the practical joke at Gad's Hill, persuasively presenting it so as to ensure Hal's involvement. Occasionally there is a suggestion that he feels a certain antagonism towards Falstaff (II, iv, 135). He has a sharp wit and is disappointed by Hal's apparently pointless joke on Francis (II, iv, 86–88).

With the honest but stupid Hostess and the dull drawer Francis, these characters are part of a distinct world whose language and manners present a strong contrast to the world of court and politics. They show us a lively carefree disorder which is, however, never too far from violence and anarchy.

A rather different view of the common people is given in Act II Scene i when we see the Two Carriers preparing for their journey. In the early morning gloom we are given a brief but illuminating glimpse

of the everyday cares of honest working people. Bad food, old horses
and lousy beds are the staple of their conversation, which uses the
earthiest and most robust colloquial idiom. It is a long way from their
world to the rarefied atmosphere of the court, yet on stage the journey
takes only an instant. In the rapid change of location and tone lies much
of the dramatic effect of *1 Henry IV*.

Commentary

HONOUR

The theme of honour, central to the development of *1 Henry IV*, is elaborated mainly through the characters of Hotspur, Falstaff and Hal. Hotspur and Falstaff represent two conceptions of honour, diametrically opposed; each interpretation lacks essential elements. In the character of Hal we see these conflicting versions of honour transcended and made into something much more valuable. In the very first scene of the play the King establishes the contrast between Hotspur – 'the theme of honour's tongue' – and his own son, whose reputation is stained by 'riot and dishonour'.

For Hotspur the pursuit of honour is the highest aim in life. Both his admirable and his deplorable qualities spring from this attitude. He is undoubtedly brave and a great soldier, as the King, Douglas and Glendower all acknowledge. He is straightforward and honest, a man of integrity; unlike his uncle Worcester, he does not cover his motives with a layer of pious deceit.

However, Hotspur's pursuit of honour proves to be dangerous, not just to himself but to the whole nation. His obsession leads him to exclude any more important consideration when deciding which course he will take. Since he wants to monopolize honour, he must defeat any possible rival – in this case, Hal. We feel that Hotspur rebels against the King because he feels his honour is threatened by the Percys' association with what he calls 'this ingrate and cankered Bolingbroke'. How, he asks his father, can you bear the stain on your reputation which you suffer from being linked with the murder of Richard II? (I, iii, 159–87). Northumberland may redeem his 'banished honours', he goes on, by overthrowing the King. Furthermore, Hotspur's pride is offended by the King's demand for his prisoners.

We notice that, for Hotspur, war is not regarded as something terrible and destructive; it is simply a means of pursuing yet more glory. At the end of Act I Scene iii he shows his immature attitude: 'O, let the hours be short/Till fields and blows and groans applaud our sport!' War is a game and the prize is honour. Even at Shrewsbury, when he wishes that the battle might be only between himself and Hal (V, ii, 47), we realize that this is not because of any desire to spare unnecessary suffering but rather to highlight the honour that is at stake.

In contrast, Falstaff shows that he regards Hotspur's kind of honour as absurd. His behaviour at Gad's Hill certainly shows that he values his safety much more than his reputation. Yet we see, in Act I I Scene iv, that Falstaff would love to be thought honourable and brave. His lies are a gross parody of true courage, and put Hotspur's ranting speeches of Act I Scene iii into perspective; Hotspur's attitude appears in a less favourable light after it has been rendered ridiculous by Falstaff's exaggerations.

Several times in Act V Falstaff explicitly states his notion of honour. In his 'catechism' (V, i, 127) he wittily reduces honour to an empty concept – it is 'a mere scutcheon' (the heraldic device displayed at funerals). For Falstaff life is valuable and must be preserved at any price. We see him running away at Gad's Hill and so we are prepared for his cowardly and cynical behaviour at Shrewsbury. He sees the brave Sir Walter Blunt's corpse and exclaims, 'There's honour for you!' Yet he confesses, a moment later, that he has deliberately allowed his men to be killed in order to line his own pockets. 'Give me life; which if I can save, so; if not, honour comes unlooked for, and there's an end.' Falstaff's version of honour licenses him to do anything so long as his own life is preserved. If we are still in doubt that Falstaff's honour is as dangerous and empty an idea as Hotspur's, then we are finally convinced by his shocking mutilation of Hotspur's corpse. The irony, of course, is that Falstaff commits this cowardly act in order to gain the rewards of the honour he despises.

Between these two extreme attitudes to honour is the figure of Hal. At the beginning of the play, as his father points out, his reputation is the very opposite of Hotspur's; he seems to have more in common with the 'riot and dishonour' associated with Falstaff. The audience learns, however, from his soliloquy in Act I Scene ii that he is not at all taken in by the tavern world. As the play progresses he becomes more disillusioned with Falstaff's lies and cowardice; his insults, which had started mainly as jokes, become more pointed and wounding. As news of the rebellion arrives (II, iv), he has seen through Falstaff and is about to 'banish' him (as he plays the role of his father). Now we see Hal distancing himself from the anarchic mock-authority figure of Falstaff. His opinion of Hotspur rises (in Act II Scene iv he had parodied Hotspur as a bloodthirsty maniac). In the reconciliation scene with his father Hal shows his high regard both for Hotspur himself and the honour he epitomizes (III, ii, 129–59).

Hal begins to present a changed public image. The rebel Vernon describes his preparations for war in terms which depict Hal as the very soul of honour and chivalry (IV, i, 97–110). He later praises, in a similar manner, Hal's delivery of the challenge to Hotspur (V, ii, 51). We should notice that on neither occasion can Hotspur bear to hear such high praise of his arch rival. Hal, on the other hand, has nothing but praise for Hotspur's gallantry and valour.

The difference between Hal and Hotspur is that Hal's attitude to honour is neither obsessive nor unreflective. He certainly wants to gain honour and defeat Hotspur, but he does not lack a sense of proportion or of the human cost of war. When Hal makes his challenge (V, i, 83) it is as much 'to save the blood on either side' as to focus attention on the climax of his rivalry with Hotspur. When Hotspur wishes for single combat with Hal we feel that he does so only because it might increase the glory for the victor.

Hal's greater humanity has been learnt, to a large extent, from Falstaff and the tavern world. Without this experience he would not have the maturity to understand the tragedy of war as well as its glory. He takes what he needs from Falstaff's and Hotspur's versions of honour and discards what is irresponsible. In battle we see him performing honourably and bravely. Yet, after defeating Hotspur, his speech over his dead rival shows a mature view of honour in which the claims of life and glory are finely balanced.

KINGSHIP

The importance of the concept of kingship in *1 Henry IV* can be inferred from the introduction, four times in the play, of the story of Henry's rise to power, once by himself and three times by the rebels (I, iii; III, ii; IV, iii and V, i). We are inevitably led to consider two questions: How is power acquired? And, once acquired, how is it used?

When the rebels give their account of how Henry became king they emphasize his treachery and ambition. They claim that the Percys supported Henry after his return from exile solely on the understanding that his ambition should be limited to regaining the lands and titles due to him by birth (Hotspur in IV, iii and Worcester in V, i). They present themselves as having been used by Henry to gain power; now that he is king, they say, he has forgotten their help and threatens their safety.

When Henry tells the story (III, ii) the emphasis is rather different. He suggests to Hal that he became king more by chance than design; the people were moved by the contrast between his regal bearing and the corruption of Richard II, who 'mingled his royalty with cap'ring fools' and 'grew a companion to the common streets'.

We must be careful to balance these versions. The Percys undoubtedly exaggerate their account, while Henry leaves much out of his. The Percys' version is distorted by their ambition and their resentment of Henry's power, while Henry is careful not to show himself in too bad a light to his son.

What we cannot forget, though, is the illegality of Henry's rise to power. Whatever the precise extent of his guilt, he has deposed the rightful king; he has committed a crime against the moral, as well as the political, order. Richard II was a weak and ineffectual ruler and as a result the country was racked by the power struggles of the greater nobles; but he was undeniably the legitimate king. The sin Henry has committed in deposing him has resulted in the present rebellion. If his ambition could dethrone Richard, why, think the Percys, can they not topple Henry?

Henry became king, though, and it is Henry's duty to rule: to maintain order and justice. As the play opens it is plain that he has not been successful; the Scots and Welsh are in arms and the Percys are unwilling to submit to his authority. He admits that he has not been authoritative enough (I, iii, 1–4) but with the direct challenge to him he assumes a more regal air: 'I will from henceforth rather be myself,/ Mighty and to be feared ...' He deals firmly with the rebels, as we see immediately by his explusion of Worcester. He acts swiftly to mobilize his forces and confront the rebels at Shrewsbury.

Henry does not lack mercy. He shows he prefers peace to civil turmoil when he makes his 'kind and liberal offer' to Worcester in Act V Scene i; we have no reason to think Worcester is right in doubting the King's sincerity. What Henry does lack, though, is warmth – the sympathy that would enable him to understand all his subjects, even the lowest inn-servant. He is a remote and rather cold figure. He teaches his son about one aspect of kingship, but it is from the mock-authority figure of Falstaff that Hal learns the warmth and sympathy that will make him a better king than his father.

THE EDUCATION OF A PRINCE

The development of Hal's character in the play is in itself an important theme, for what emerges is an account of the education of a prince. His story is not just that of any young man in the process of growing up, but of a future monarch learning what his responsibilities are.

Hal's schooling takes place in the context of two opposed worlds; his father and the court are balanced by Falstaff and the tavern. From his father Hal learns about the heavy burden that lies upon a king. As he sees Henry dealing with the rebellion he recognizes the necessity for firm authority in maintaining order.

But Henry, as we have said, is a remote and rather cold figure. This absence of human warmth is what Hal makes up for by his experiences with Falstaff and the tavern. Thus when Hal comes to move away from the irresponsibility of his tavern companions he has learned a sympathy that will be invaluable to him as king. In Act II Scene iv he describes his drinking with the drawers who take him for 'a lad of mettle, a good boy'; he has learned an easy manner which enables him to move comfortably between the very different worlds of nobleman and commoner.

By the end of the play Hal has become capable of serious thought about the nation's government. He has assumed his responsibilities and shown great qualities of leadership and courage. All this would not have been possible had he not added the humanity of the tavern world to his father's authority.

Hal's education, though, is not complete by the end of *1 Henry IV*. When he promises to 'gild' Falstaff's lie about having killed Hotspur he still retains a great affection for the rogue. It is only in the second part of *Henry IV*, with the rebellion crushed and his father dead, that Hal completes his education by ascending the throne.

Examination Questions

1. Read the following passage, and answer all the questions printed beneath it:

FALSTAFF I am accursed to rob in that thief's company; the rascal hath removed my horse and tied him I know not where. If I travel but four foot by the square further afoot I shall break my wind. Well, I doubt not but to die a fair death for all this, if I 'scape hanging for killing that rogue. I have forsworn his company hourly any time 5 this two-and-twenty years, and yet I am bewitched with the rogue's company. If the rascal have not given me medicines to make me love him, I'll be hanged: it could not be else: I have drunk medicines. Poins! Hal! a plague upon you both! Bardolph! Peto! I'll starve ere I'll rob a foot further. An 'twere not as good a deed as drink to turn 10 true man and leave these rogues, I am the veriest varlet that ever chewed with a tooth. Eight yards of uneven ground is threescore and ten miles afoot with me, and the stony-hearted villains know it well enough. A plague upon't when thieves cannot be true one to another! (*They whistle.*) Whew! A plague upon you all! Give me my horse, 15 you rogues; give me my horse and be hanged.

PRINCE (*coming forward*) Peace, ye fatguts! lie down: lay thine ear close to the ground, and list if thou canst hear the tread of travellers.

FALSTAFF Have you any levers to lift me up again, being down? 'Sblood! I'll not bear mine own flesh so far afoot again for all the 20 coin in thy father's exchequer. What a plague mean ye to colt me thus?

PRINCE Thou liest: thou art not colted; thou art uncolted.

FALSTAFF I prithee, good Prince Hal, help me to my horse, good king's son. 25

PRINCE Out, you rogue! shall I be your ostler?

FALSTAFF Go, hang thyself in thine own heir apparent garters! If I be ta'en I'll peach for this.

(i) What are the circumstances in which this exchange takes place?

(ii) Bring out in your own words the meaning of *I have drunk medicines* (line 8); *I'll starve ere I'll rob a foot further* (lines 9–10); *thou art not colted*; *thou art uncolted* (line 23); *If I be ta'en I'll peach for this* (line 28).

(iii) What do you find amusing in the passage?

(*University of Oxford Local Examination Board, 1978*)

2. Read the following passage, and answer all the questions printed beneath it:

WORCESTER The Prince of Wales stepp'd forth before the king,
    And, nephew, challeng'd you to single fight.
HOTSPUR O! would the quarrel lay upon our heads,
    And that no man might draw short breath today
    But I and Harry Monmouth. Tell me, tell me,   5
    How show'd his tasking? seem'd it in contempt?
VERNON No, by my soul; I never in my life
    Did hear a challenge urg'd more modestly,
    Unless a brother should a brother dare
    To gentle exercise and proof of arms.   10
    He gave you all the duties of a man,
    Trimm'd up your praises with a princely tongue,
    Spoke your deservings like a chronicle,
    Making you ever better than his praise,
    By still dispraising praise valu'd with you;   15
    And, which became him like a prince indeed,
    He made a blushing cital of himself,
    And chid his truant youth with such a grace
    As if he master'd there a double spirit
    Of teaching and of learning instantly.   20

> There did he pause. But let me tell the world,
> If he outlive the envy of this day,
> England did never owe so sweet a hope,
> So much misconstru'd in his wantonness.
> HOTSPUR Cousin, I think thou art enamoured   25
> On his follies: never did I hear
> Of any prince so wild a libertine.
> But be he as he will, yet once ere night
> I will embrace him with a soldier's arm,
> That he shall shrink under my courtesy.   30

(i) Bring out in your own words the meaning of lines 17–20 (*He made a blushing cital ... of learning instantly*).

(ii) What do you learn of Hotspur from his speeches in this passage?

(iii) What impressions of Prince Henry do you get from this passage?

(*University of Oxford Local Examination Board, 1978*)

3. Either, (*a*) Give an account of that part of Act II Scene iv, in which Prince Henry and Poins expose Falstaff's lies about his exploits at Gadshill, and the Prince and Falstaff enact interviews between the Prince and his father.

Or, (*b*) 'A hare-brain'd Hotspur, govern'd by a spleen': is this an adequate description of Hotspur?

Or, (*c*) Show how Shakespeare relieves the gravity of the historical events of the play by means of humour.

(*University of Oxford Local Examination Board, 1978*)

4. By close reference to their speeches and actions, contrast the attitudes towards honour of Hotspur, the Prince and Falstaff.

(*University of London Schools Examinations Board, 1976*)

5. 'The King is a lonely figure, a bitter and broken man.' Write a study of the King, referring to the above comment and making clear your own view of him.

(*University of London Schools Examinations Board, 1976*)

6. Explain fully why the Percy family (Worcester, Northumberland and Hotspur) rebelled against the King. To what extent, in your opinion, did their own characters contribute to their defeat?

(*University of London Schools Examination Board, 1976*)

7. Give an account of the Gad's Hill robbery and its sequel in the Boar's Head Tavern (up to the announcement by the Hostess of the arrival of the nobleman from the court), bringing out the points which make this episode in the play outstandingly humorous.

(*University of London Schools Examination Board, 1976*)

8. 'Compared with Falstaff on the one hand and Hotspur on the other, the Prince emerges as a shadowy and unattractive figure.' What is your view?

(*Oxford and Cambridge Schools Examination Board, 1970*)

9. What indications are there in the play that Prince Hal will later become a strong and serious-minded king?

(*Oxford and Cambridge Schools Examination Board, 1974*)

10. Prince Hal in jest calls Falstaff 'the bolting hutch of beastliness'; do you think that Shakespeare intended us to see Falstaff as more than just a fat buffoon?

(*Oxford and Cambridge Schools Examination Board, 1974*)

11. Prince Hal said that were it not for laughing at Falstaff he would pity him. How far do you agree with this view of Falstaff?

(Oxford and Cambridge Schools Examination Board, 1974)

12. 'The young Prince Hal was by no means a satisfactory son, but neither was the King a very good father.' What is your view?

(Oxford and Cambridge Schools Examination Board, 1974)

13. How far does Shakespeare persuade us that the reason for the defeat of the rebels at Shrewsbury was mainly due to faults in the characters of their leaders?

(Oxford and Cambridge Schools Examination Board, 1974)

14. What do Falstaff's low companions contribute to the play?

(Oxford and Cambridge Schools Examination Board, 1974)

PENGUIN PASSNOTES

Already published

Penguin Examination Bestsellers

Jane Austen/Pride and Prejudice

H. E. Bates/Fair Stood the Wind for France

Charlotte Brontë/Jane Eyre

Emily Brontë/Wuthering Heights

Charles Dickens/Great Expectations

Gerald Durrell/My Family and Other Animals

George Eliot/Silas Marner

Oliver Goldsmith/The Vicar of Wakefield

Graham Greene/Brighton Rock

Graham Greene/The Power and the Glory

Thomas Hardy/Far From the Madding Crowd

Thomas Hardy/The Mayor of Casterbridge

L.P. Hartley/The Go-Between

Barry Hines/A Kestrel for a Knave

Geoffrey Household/Rogue Male

A Choice of Penguins

The Heart of the Matter
GRAHAM GREENE

Scobie, a police officer in a flyblown West African colony during the war, is above suspicion.

Then, passed over for promotion, he is forced to borrow money from a Syrian trader to send his faded wife Louise on holiday.

In her absence, he falls in love with a pathetic child widow ... and, inexorably, his conscience and his love of God lead him to disaster.

'Graham Greene is one of the finest living writers in English' – *Scotsman*

Love for Lydia
H. E. BATES

'All the happiness and the sorrow of young people in love is put in its correct perspective by the maturity and skill of a born storyteller' – Alan Melville

Lydia, a girl from a wealthy but isolated background, gradually discovers the delights of growing up – completely captivating the young men who are her companions

The lives of the young people unfold against the carefree background of the late twenties, with summers at their hottest and winters at their coldest. It is a glimpse back at an age not long gone, but nonetheless gone forever.

A Choice of Penguins

A Summer Bird-Cage
MARGARET DRABBLE

Living, working and party-going in London . . .
Two sisters. Bright, attractive Sarah, newly down from
Oxford and now bed-sittering in Highbury; and beautiful Louise,
who has just made a brilliant marriage to the rich but unlikeable
novelist Stephen Halifax.

But (despite their strangely protracted continental honeymoon)
things seem to be going badly wrong . . . if the enigmatic letters, the
hints dropped at parties and the bitchy newspaper gossip are
anything to go by.

As the situation reaches its bizarre climax, Louise and Sarah too
have to discover whether they can really forgive each other
for existing.

'She is one of the best . . . and one of the most read and
best-known novelists now writing' –
Guardian

Odd Girl Out
ELIZABETH JANE HOWARD

Anne and Edmund Cornhill have a happy marriage and a lovely
home. They are content, complete, absorbed in their private idyll.

Arabella, who comes to stay one lazy summer, is rich, rootless
and amoral – and, as they find out, beautiful and loving.

With her elegant prose the author traces the web of love and
desire that entangles these three; but it is Arabella who finally
loses out.

Elizabeth Jane Howard reveals with devastating accuracy a
situation both shattering and destructive.